GOLANG PROGRAMMING FOR BEGINNERS

A BEGINNER'S BLUEPRINT TO BUILDING APPS AND UNLOCKING CODING SUCCESS

SIMON TELLIER

TABLE OF CONTENTS

PREFACE

Why I Wrote This Book

Learning to program can feel overwhelming, especially when trying to choose the right language. Beginners often get stuck between choices—Python, JavaScript, C++, Rust—without knowing which will truly serve their long-term goals. Go (or Golang) is often overlooked by newcomers because it's not as hyped as some other languages. But in reality, Go is one of the most powerful, efficient, and beginner-friendly programming languages available today.

I wrote this book because I've seen many beginners struggle with overly technical books that assume too much knowledge. Most programming resources either start with complex theoretical concepts or skip critical foundational topics, leaving beginners feeling lost. My goal is to create a book that **bridges that gap**—one that teaches Go from the ground up while keeping things **clear, practical, and engaging**.

Go was designed by some of the world's best engineers at Google to solve real-world programming challenges, yet it remains **simple enough for a beginner to grasp**. Unlike some other languages, Go has a clean syntax, built-in concurrency support, and a thriving ecosystem for building everything from command-line tools to web applications and cloud services. More importantly, Go developers are in **high demand**, making it a great choice for those looking to break into software development or expand their skills.

If you're just starting out and want to **learn how to build practical applications quickly**—without getting bogged down by unnecessary theory—this book is for you. My goal is to guide you **step by step** so you can **write real Go programs with confidence** by the time you finish.

Who This Book Is For

This book is designed for **absolute beginners** who have little or no experience with Go or programming in general. However, if you already have some experience with other languages like Python, JavaScript, or Java and want to add Go to your skill set, you'll also find plenty of value here.

This book is for you if:

✔ You're completely new to programming and want a **clear, structured** way to start.
✔ You've tried learning to code before but found most resources **too complex** or overwhelming.
✔ You're an experienced developer looking to **learn Go quickly and efficiently**.
✔ You want to build real-world applications like **web apps, REST APIs, or command-line tools**.
✔ You're interested in Go's **performance benefits and concurrency features**.

Who This Book Is NOT For?

✘ If you're looking for an advanced deep dive into Go's internals or compiler design, this book won't cover those topics in-depth.
✘ If you prefer a purely theoretical approach without hands-on coding, this book takes a more practical path.
✘ If you need a quick reference guide rather than a **step-by-step learning resource**, this book might be too detailed for your needs.

This book is designed to take you from **zero to a functional Go programmer** by focusing on **real projects and hands-on coding exercises**. If that sounds like what you need, then you're in the right place.

What You Will Learn

This book is structured to provide a **gradual, practical learning experience**. We'll start with **absolute basics** and build toward **real-world projects**. By the end of the book, you'll be able to:

- **Understand the fundamentals** of Go, including its syntax, variables, loops, and functions.
- **Write clean and efficient Go programs** using best practices.
- **Work with data structures**, including slices, maps, and structs.
- **Understand Go's unique approach to error handling** (without relying on exceptions like other languages).
- **Master Go's built-in concurrency features**, including goroutines and channels.
- **Build a command-line tool** to automate tasks.
- **Develop a REST API** using Go's net/http package.
- **Write and test Go code effectively** to catch and prevent bugs.
- **Deploy your Go applications** and make them production-ready.

We'll also **work on small projects** throughout the book to reinforce learning, culminating in a **full-fledged web application** that ties everything together.

How to Get the Most Out of This Book

1. Code Along With the Examples

This book isn't just about **reading**—it's about **doing**. Programming is best learned by **writing code**, so I encourage you to **follow along, type out the examples**, and test things on your own machine.

Each chapter includes practical exercises and projects that reinforce what you've learned. If you get stuck, don't hesitate to tweak the code, break things, and experiment—**this is the best way to learn**.

---

2. Don't Rush—Learn Step by Step

Go has a **simple syntax**, but like any programming language, it takes time to master. Instead of trying to memorize everything, focus on **understanding concepts** and **applying them through hands-on practice**.

Each chapter builds upon the previous one, so take your time and **progress at your own pace**. If something isn't clear, re-read the section, try writing your own examples, or look at the additional exercises at the end of each chapter.

---

3. Test Yourself With Challenges

Throughout the book, you'll find **challenges and exercises** designed to help you think critically and apply what you've learned. These aren't just for practice—they help **reinforce concepts** and ensure you're truly grasping the material.

Don't skip them! Even if they seem tough at first, working through challenges will make you **a better developer**.

---

4. Ask Questions and Keep Learning

No programmer learns everything in a single book—learning to code is an ongoing process. The Go community is **friendly and welcoming**, so don't hesitate to ask questions, whether through online forums, GitHub, or Go-related communities like:

- **Go's official forum:** forum.golang.org
- **The Go subreddit:** r/golang
- **Stack Overflow (Go tag)**

Additionally, I've included **recommended resources** at the end of the book to help you continue learning after you've finished reading.

---

5. Build Something On Your Own

By the time you finish this book, you'll have enough knowledge to **build and deploy your own Go applications**. Don't stop here—pick an idea you're passionate about and start coding!

Whether it's a **web app, a game, a tool for automating tasks, or an API**, applying your knowledge to a real-world project is the best way to solidify your skills and gain confidence as a developer.

Final Thoughts

Programming with Go is one of the most **rewarding skills** you can learn, whether you're aiming to **start a new career**, **build your own projects**, or simply **level up as a developer**. This book is designed to make that journey **clear, practical, and enjoyable**.

So, let's **start coding in Go!** 🚀

Chapter 1: Introduction to Go (Golang)

What is Go? A Brief History and Evolution

Go, often referred to as **Golang**, is a modern programming language designed for **simplicity, efficiency, and performance**. It was created by **Robert Griesemer, Rob Pike, and Ken Thompson** at Google in **2007** and officially released in **2009**.

The motivation behind Go stemmed from the **frustrations** that the Google engineers faced while working with large-scale systems using languages like C++ and Java. They found these languages **too slow to compile, too complex**, and **too verbose** for the kind of high-performance, scalable applications they needed.

The Key Problems Go Was Created to Solve

1. **Slow Compilation** – Traditional languages like C++ took **too long to compile** large codebases, making development sluggish.
2. **Excessive Complexity** – Features like inheritance and manual memory management in older languages made code **harder to maintain**.
3. **Concurrency Challenges** – Handling **multiple tasks at once (parallel execution)** was difficult and error-prone in C, C++, and Java.
4. **Inefficient Garbage Collection** – Some languages required **manual memory management**, leading to **bugs and performance issues**.

With these challenges in mind, Go was built to be:

- **Fast** – It compiles quickly, making development smoother.
- **Simple** – The syntax is **straightforward and easy to read**.
- **Efficient** – It handles **concurrency** better than many other languages.
- **Safe** – It has **automatic memory management**, reducing memory leaks.

How Go Has Evolved

Since its launch in **2009**, Go has become **one of the most widely used programming languages in the world**. Major tech companies, including **Google, Uber, Dropbox, Netflix, and Twitch**, use Go to build highly scalable, high-performance applications.

Key milestones in Go's development:
- **2009** – Initial release of Go 1.0.
- **2012** – Google starts using Go in production.
- **2015** – Go gains popularity as a backend language for web applications.
- **2019** – Go 1.13 introduces improved error handling and performance updates.
- **2023** – Go 1.20+ features enhanced **generics, memory improvements, and security fixes**.

Today, **Go is one of the top choices** for cloud computing, backend services, web APIs, and even blockchain applications.

Why Go? Understanding Its Advantages

If you're new to programming, you might wonder, **"Why should I learn Go instead of Python, Java, or JavaScript?"**

The answer lies in **Go's unique strengths**. Unlike many other programming languages, **Go was designed for modern computing needs**—offering a **perfect balance** of speed, simplicity, and reliability.

1. Go is Easy to Learn and Read

- **Minimalist syntax** – Go's language design is **simple** compared to C++ or Java.

- **No unnecessary complexity** – No **classes, no exceptions, no deep inheritance trees**.
- **Consistency** – Go has an **opinionated style** (with gofmt formatting), making all Go code look uniform across different projects.

This simplicity makes Go an **excellent choice for beginners** while also being powerful enough for large-scale applications.

---

2. Go is Fast (Almost as Fast as C and C++)

- Go **compiles directly to machine code**, making it **much faster than interpreted languages** like Python and JavaScript.
- Unlike Java, **Go does not require a virtual machine (JVM)**, which reduces runtime overhead.
- Benchmarks show that **Go is almost as fast as C**, making it ideal for performance-critical applications.

Real-World Example:
Cloud services like **Google Cloud and Kubernetes** use Go because of its speed and efficiency.

---

3. Go is Great for Concurrency (Multi-Threading)

- **Go was built with concurrency in mind.**
- Unlike Python or Java, which require complex threading, Go **natively supports lightweight threads called Goroutines**.
- Goroutines allow Go programs to run **multiple tasks simultaneously** without consuming too many system resources.

Example:

A Go-based **web server can handle thousands of users** simultaneously with **minimal memory usage**—something difficult to achieve in other languages without advanced multithreading techniques.

---

4. Go is Used by Top Tech Companies

Major companies use Go because of its **scalability, simplicity, and speed**.

Company	Use Case
Google	Cloud computing services, Kubernetes
Uber	High-performance backend services
Netflix	Content delivery and real-time analytics
Twitch	Video streaming and chat services
Dropbox	Cloud storage infrastructure

If you're looking to **work in the tech industry**, learning Go can give you a **huge advantage**.

---

5. Go is Open Source and Backed by Google

- Go is **free** and open-source, with a **large and active developer community**.
- Google, one of the most powerful tech companies, **actively maintains and improves** Go.
- Regular updates keep Go **secure, stable, and modern**.

---

6. Go is Versatile (Not Just for Web Development!)

Most people associate Go with backend development, but it's capable of much more:

- **Web development** – Build REST APIs, microservices, and web servers.
- **Cloud computing** – Used in **Kubernetes, Docker, and Terraform**.
- **Command-line tools** – Many DevOps tools (like kubectl) are built with Go.
- **Blockchain and crypto** – Many crypto projects, including Ethereum's Geth client, use Go.
- **Machine learning** – Go has libraries like Gorgonia for AI applications.

This versatility means **learning Go opens up multiple career opportunities**.

---

7. Go Makes Deployment Simple

Unlike languages like Python or Java, where you must **install dependencies** and configure environments, Go **compiles to a single executable binary**.

This means:

- You can **run a Go program on any OS** (Linux, Windows, Mac) without extra setup.
- Deploying a Go application is as simple as **copying one file**.
- This makes Go an **excellent choice for cloud-based and containerized applications**.

---

8. Go's Standard Library is Powerful

Go has a **rich standard library** that includes:

- **Networking tools** (net/http) for building web apps and APIs.
- **Database connectivity** (database/sql) for working with PostgreSQL, MySQL, etc.
- **Concurrency tools** (sync, context) for managing Goroutines.
- **File handling** (os, io) for reading and writing files.

Unlike Python or JavaScript, **Go doesn't rely on third-party libraries** for most common tasks.

Go is one of the **best languages to learn today**—whether you're a **beginner** looking for an easy-to-learn language or a **developer** wanting to build **fast, scalable applications**.

■ **Simple, readable syntax**
■ **Blazing fast performance**
■ **Concurrency without headaches**
■ **Powerful standard library**
■ **Used by Google, Uber, Netflix, and more**
■ **Great for web development, cloud computing, and DevOps**

Comparing Go with Python, JavaScript, and Rust

Go is a modern programming language that competes with some of the most widely used languages today, including Python, JavaScript, and Rust. Each of these languages has strengths and weaknesses, and understanding how Go compares to them will help you see where it shines.

Go vs. Python

Python is one of the most popular programming languages, especially for beginners, data science, and web development. However, Go has some key advantages over Python, particularly in performance and scalability.

Feature	Go ⚪	Python
Ease of Learning	Simple syntax, but requires learning some new concepts like Goroutines	Very beginner-friendly with readable syntax
Performance	Much faster than Python (compiled language)	Slower due to being an interpreted language
Concurrency	Built-in concurrency support with Goroutines	Multi-threading is complex and requires extra libraries
Use Cases	Web development, APIs, backend services, DevOps, cloud computing	Web development, data science, scripting, automation
Error Handling	Explicit error handling (no exceptions)	Uses exceptions for error handling
Scalability	Great for large-scale applications	Can struggle with high-concurrency workloads

- ◆ **Verdict:**

If you want to work in machine learning, AI, or data science, Python is the better choice. However, for backend systems, web services, and high-performance applications, Go is much faster and more efficient than Python.

Go vs. JavaScript

JavaScript is the most widely used language for web development. However, JavaScript (and its backend runtime, Node.js) has some drawbacks that Go addresses.

Feature	Go ◯	JavaScript (Node.js) ⚡
Performance	Much faster (compiled)	Slower than Go (interpreted)
Concurrency	Goroutines provide true parallel execution	Uses an event loop (async/await) but lacks true parallelism
Use Cases	Backend services, APIs, cloud computing, DevOps	Web apps, APIs, front-end development
Typing	Statically typed (fewer runtime errors)	Dynamically typed (more prone to errors)
Error Handling	Explicit error handling	Uses try/catch blocks for exceptions
Scalability	Highly scalable due to Goroutines	Can struggle under high concurrency

• Verdict:

For frontend web development, JavaScript is the clear winner since Go isn't designed for browsers. However, for backend development, APIs, and performance-heavy applications, Go is significantly faster and more scalable than Node.js.

Go vs. Rust

Rust is often compared to Go because both are modern systems-level languages. However, they serve different purposes.

Feature	Go 🔵	Rust 🦀
Ease of Learning	Easier to learn and write	More complex, steep learning curve
Performance	High speed, but not as fast as Rust	One of the fastest languages, even faster than Go
Memory Management	Garbage collected (easier for beginners)	Manual memory management (safer but more complex)
Concurrency	Simple with Goroutines	Powerful but requires learning borrowing and ownership concepts
Use Cases	Web services, cloud computing, APIs, DevOps	Systems programming, embedded systems, game engines, security-sensitive applications

- **Verdict:**

If you need maximum performance and low-level control, Rust is better. However, for fast development and easier concurrency, Go is the more practical choice.

Who Uses Go? Real-World Examples

Go has been widely adopted by some of the biggest tech companies due to its performance, scalability, and ease of development. Let's look at some of the major players that rely on Go.

1. Google

Go was created at Google, so it's no surprise that Google uses it for many of its internal and external projects.

- Google services powered by Go:

  - Kubernetes – The world's leading container orchestration platform.
  - Google Cloud Platform (GCP) – Various cloud-based services use Go.
  - Dagger.io – Google's internal tools for infrastructure management.

Why Google chose Go:

- Fast performance
- Built-in concurrency for handling massive traffic
- Easy deployment and maintenance

---

2. Uber

Uber handles millions of ride requests per day, requiring a high-performance, low-latency backend system.

- How Uber uses Go:

  - Geo-fencing system – Go helps manage Uber's real-time location tracking and pricing system.
  - Marketplace service – Handles trip matching and fare calculations.

Why Uber chose Go:

- High-speed data processing
- Better scalability than Python
- Easy maintenance with a small codebase

---

3. Netflix

Netflix delivers huge amounts of video content to users worldwide and requires an efficient backend to manage streaming, recommendations, and analytics.

- How Netflix uses Go:

  - Distributed caching – Helps deliver content faster.
  - Performance monitoring – Go-based services track system health.

Why Netflix chose Go:

- High concurrency
- Low memory footprint
- Improved API performance

---

4. Dropbox

Dropbox switched from Python to Go to improve performance and reduce infrastructure costs.

- How Dropbox uses Go:

  - Storage infrastructure – Optimized file storage and synchronization.
  - API services – Faster handling of file uploads and sharing.

Why Dropbox chose Go:

- Python was too slow for their needs.
- Go improved CPU usage and response times.
- Reduced server costs by 50%.

---

5. Twitch

Twitch, the world's largest game streaming platform, needs low-latency chat services and scalable backend architecture.

- ◆ How Twitch uses Go:

  - Chat system – Handles millions of concurrent users.
  - Data pipelines – Processes streaming analytics in real-time.

Why Twitch chose Go:

- Handles millions of concurrent connections.
- Goroutines allow efficient event handling.

---

6. Cloudflare

Cloudflare, a global content delivery network (CDN) and security provider, uses Go for its high-performance networking solutions.

- ◆ How Cloudflare uses Go:

  - DDoS protection – Handles high traffic and cyber threats efficiently.
  - API gateway services – Speeds up website load times.

Why Cloudflare chose Go:

- Low-latency performance.
- Simple, maintainable codebase.

Go has proven to be one of the best languages for modern software development. It's used by startups and tech giants alike because of its performance, simplicity, and scalability.

Why should you learn Go?

■ Beginner-friendly, yet powerful

■ Used by top companies (Google, Uber, Netflix, etc.)

■ Perfect for high-performance, scalable applications

■ Great for web development, APIs, cloud computing, and DevOps

■ Offers built-in concurrency (no headaches with multi-threading!)

Now that you understand why Go is a great choice, let's move on to setting up your Go environment and writing your first Go program! 🚀

Installing Go on Windows, macOS, and Linux

Before writing our first Go program, we need to install Go on your system. The installation process is straightforward and takes just a few minutes.

Step 1: Download Go

Go's official website provides the latest version of Go for all major operating systems.

1. Open your browser and go to the official Go download page:
   👉 https://go.dev/dl/
2. Choose the version for your operating system:
   ○ Windows: .msi installer
   ○ macOS: .pkg installer
   ○ Linux: .tar.gz archive

Installing Go on Windows

Step 1: Run the Installer

1. Download the .msi installer from the official Go website.
2. Double-click the installer and follow the setup instructions.
3. Choose the installation directory (default is C:\Go).

Step 2: Configure Environment Variables

After installation, we need to ensure Go is available in the system's PATH.

Open Command Prompt (cmd) or PowerShell and type:

sh

CopyEdit

go version

1. If Go is installed correctly, you should see the installed Go version.
2. To manually add Go to PATH (if necessary):
   - Open System Properties → Advanced → Environment Variables.
   - Find Path under System Variables, select it, and click Edit.
   - Add this path: C:\Go\bin.
   - Click OK and restart your terminal.

Step 3: Verify Installation

Run:

sh

CopyEdit

go version

If the installation was successful, you'll see something like:

bash

CopyEdit

go version go1.21.4 windows/amd64

Installing Go on macOS

Step 1: Install Using the .pkg Installer

1. **Download the macOS .pkg installer from the official Go website.**
2. **Open the downloaded file and follow the installation instructions.**
3. **Go is installed in /usr/local/go by default.**

Step 2: Configure the PATH Variable

To make sure Go is recognized by the terminal, open Terminal and add Go's bin directory to your shell profile:

For zsh (macOS default shell):

sh

CopyEdit

```
echo 'export PATH=$PATH:/usr/local/go/bin' >> ~/.zshrc
source ~/.zshrc
```

For bash users:

sh

CopyEdit

```
echo 'export PATH=$PATH:/usr/local/go/bin' >> ~/.bash_profile
source ~/.bash_profile
```

Step 3: Verify Installation

Run:

sh

CopyEdit

```
go version
```

You should see output similar to:

bash

CopyEdit

go version go1.21.4 darwin/amd64

Installing Go on Linux

Step 1: Download and Extract Go

Open a terminal and run:

sh

CopyEdit

wget https://go.dev/dl/go1.21.4.linux-amd64.tar.gz

1. *(Replace 1.21.4 with the latest version from the Go website.)*

Extract the archive to /usr/local:

sh

CopyEdit

sudo tar -C /usr/local -xzf go1.21.4.linux-amd64.tar.gz

2. Step 2: Add Go to PATH

To make Go accessible system-wide, add it to your profile:

For bash users:

sh

CopyEdit

```
echo 'export PATH=$PATH:/usr/local/go/bin' >> ~/.bashrc

source ~/.bashrc
```

For zsh users:

sh

CopyEdit

```
echo 'export PATH=$PATH:/usr/local/go/bin' >> ~/.zshrc

source ~/.zshrc
```

Step 3: Verify Installation

Run:

sh

CopyEdit

```
go version
```

You should see output like:

bash

CopyEdit

go version go1.21.4 linux/amd64

Now, Go is successfully installed on your system! 🎉

Setting Up Your First Go Project

Now that Go is installed, let's create our first Go program.

Understanding the Go Workspace

Go follows a structured workspace layout, but unlike older versions that required a GOPATH, modern Go (1.11+) supports Go Modules, making project management much simpler.

A typical Go project looks like this:

bash

CopyEdit

/my-go-project

| — go.mod

| — main.go

| — README.md

```
|—— /pkg

|—— /cmd

|—— /internal

|—— /scripts
```

For now, let's keep things simple and create a basic project.

Step 1: Create a New Go Project

Open a terminal and navigate to your desired project directory:
sh
CopyEdit

```
mkdir my-go-project

cd my-go-project
```

1. Initialize a new Go module:
   sh
   CopyEdit
   ```
   go mod init my-go-project
   ```

2. This creates a go.mod file, which helps manage dependencies.

Step 2: Write Your First Go Program

Inside your project folder, create a new file called main.go:

sh

CopyEdit

```
touch main.go
```

Open main.go in a text editor and add the following code:

go

CopyEdit

```go
package main

import "fmt"

func main() {

    fmt.Println("Hello, Go!")

}
```

Step 3: Run Your Go Program

To execute the program, run:

sh

CopyEdit

```sh
go run main.go
```

Output:

CopyEdit

Hello, Go!

Congratulations! 🎉 You've just written and executed your first Go program.

Breaking Down the Code

Let's go through what each part of the code does:

1. package main

Go programs are organized into packages. The main package is special—it tells Go that this is an executable program, not a library.

2. import "fmt"

Go uses import statements to include functionality from other packages.

- **The fmt package provides functions for printing output to the console.**

3. func main() {}

- **The main function is the entry point of every Go program.**
- **When the program runs, Go executes the main function first.**

4. fmt.Println("Hello, Go!")

- **fmt.Println is a built-in function that prints text to the console.**

Compiling Your Go Program

So far, we used go run, which interprets and runs the code without creating an executable. If you want to generate an actual executable file, use:

sh

CopyEdit

```
go build
```

This creates a binary file in the same directory:

go

CopyEdit

```
my-go-project/
|—— go.mod
|—— main.go
|—— my-go-project (compiled binary)
```

You can now run it like a normal program:

sh

CopyEdit

```
./my-go-project
```

Output:

CopyEdit

Hello, Go!

On Windows, the compiled file will be my-go-project.exe.

Setting Up a Go Development Environment

To make development easier, install a code editor with Go support:

■ **VS Code (Recommended)** – Install the Go extension for syntax highlighting, auto-completion, and debugging.

■ **JetBrains GoLand** – A paid but powerful Go IDE.

■ **Vim or Neovim** – If you prefer a lightweight editor.

You've now:

✔ Installed Go on your system

✔ Created and ran your first Go program

✔ Learned about Go's workspace and project structure

✔ Compiled a Go program into an executable

This foundation sets you up for the next steps—writing more advanced Go programs! 🚀

Chapter 2: Writing Your First Go Program

Now that you have Go installed and set up, it's time to start writing real Go programs. In this chapter, we'll cover the **basic syntax of Go**, walk through the **Go development workflow**, and help you understand how Go programs are structured. By the end, you'll be comfortable writing and running Go code on your own.

Understanding Go's Basic Syntax

Go's syntax is designed to be **simple, readable, and efficient**. Unlike languages with heavy use of symbols (like C++ or Rust), Go keeps things clean and minimal. Let's go over the key elements of Go's syntax with examples.

---

1. Go Programs Start with a Package Declaration

Every Go program belongs to a **package**. A package is a collection of related Go files.

- **Executable programs** must have the package main.
- **Libraries** and reusable code can use other package names.

Example:

go
CopyEdit
package main

This tells Go that this file is part of the **main package** and can be compiled into an executable program.

---

2. Importing Packages

Go programs often use **imported packages** to extend functionality. The standard library provides many useful built-in packages.

Example:

go
CopyEdit
```
import "fmt"  // Imports the fmt package for formatted output
```

You can import multiple packages at once using parentheses:

go
CopyEdit
```
import (
    "fmt"
    "math"
)
```

---

3. The main Function

Every Go program must have a main function. This is where execution starts.

Example:

go

CopyEdit

```go
func main() {
    fmt.Println("Hello, Go!")
}
```

- func defines a **function**.
- main() is the **entry point** of the program.
- fmt.Println is a **built-in function** that prints output to the console.

---

4. Variables and Constants

Go is **statically typed**, meaning variable types are determined at compile time.

Declaring Variables

go

CopyEdit

```go
var name string = "Alice"
var age int = 25
```

Go also allows **type inference**, so you can omit the type:

go

CopyEdit

```go
name := "Alice"  // Go automatically infers that name is a string
age := 25        // Go infers that age is an int
```

- := is the **short variable declaration operator**, useful for quick assignments.

Declaring Constants

Constants are **immutable** (unchangeable once assigned).

go

CopyEdit

```
const pi = 3.14
```

---

5. Data Types in Go

Go has several built-in data types:

Type	Example	Description
Integers	`int, int8, int16, int32, int64`	Whole numbers
Floats	`float32, float64`	Decimal numbers
Strings	`"Hello"`	Text
Booleans	`true, false`	True/False values
Arrays	`[5]int{1, 2, 3, 4, 5}`	Fixed-length list
Slices	`[]int{1, 2, 3, 4, 5}`	Dynamic list
Maps	`map[string]int{"Alice": 25, "Bob": 30}`	Key-value store

Example:

go

CopyEdit

```
var isGolangFun bool = true
fmt.Println(isGolangFun)  // Output: true
```

6. Control Flow (Conditionals and Loops)

Conditional Statements

go

CopyEdit

```
if age >= 18 {
    fmt.Println("You are an adult")
} else {
    fmt.Println("You are a minor")
}
```

Go also supports switch statements:

go

CopyEdit

```
switch day := "Monday"; day {
case "Monday":
    fmt.Println("Start of the week")
case "Friday":
    fmt.Println("Weekend is near")
default:
    fmt.Println("A regular day")
}
```

Loops (The for Loop)

Go **only has for loops** (no while or do-while loops).

go

CopyEdit

```go
for i := 1; i <= 5; i++ {
    fmt.Println(i)
}
```

For infinite loops:

go

CopyEdit

```go
for {
    fmt.Println("This will run forever!")
}
```

---

7. Functions in Go

Functions are **reusable blocks of code**.

go

CopyEdit

```go
func add(x int, y int) int {
    return x + y
}
```

Calling the function:

go

CopyEdit

```
sum := add(5, 3)
fmt.Println(sum)  // Output: 8
```

The Go Development Workflow

Understanding Go's workflow will help you **write, compile, and run Go programs efficiently**.

---

1. Writing Go Code

Go code is typically written in a **text editor or IDE** like:

- **Visual Studio Code** (with the Go extension)
- **GoLand** (JetBrains)
- **Vim/Neovim** (for terminal users)

Go source files use the .go extension.

---

2. Running a Go Program (Without Compilation)

You don't always need to compile Go manually. You can run Go files directly using:

sh

CopyEdit

```
go run main.go
```

This **compiles and executes** the program in one step.

---

3. Compiling a Go Program

To generate an **executable file**, use:

sh
CopyEdit

```
go build main.go
```

This creates a compiled binary (main or main.exe on Windows), which you can run:

sh
CopyEdit

```
./main
```

---

4. Formatting Go Code (gofmt)

Go has a built-in tool called gofmt that **automatically formats** your code.

To format your code:

sh
CopyEdit

```
gofmt -w main.go
```

This keeps all Go code **consistent** across different projects.

5. Managing Dependencies (go mod)

Modern Go uses **Go Modules** for dependency management.

To initialize a new project:

sh

CopyEdit

```
go mod init my-go-project
```

This creates a go.mod file to **track dependencies**.

To add a third-party package:

sh

CopyEdit

```
go get github.com/gorilla/mux
```

This installs the package and updates go.mod and go.sum.

---

6. Running Tests in Go

Go has a built-in testing framework. To create a test file, name it filename_test.go.

Example:

go

CopyEdit

```
package main

import "testing"

func TestAdd(t *testing.T) {
    result := add(2, 3)
    expected := 5

    if result != expected {
        t.Errorf("Expected %d but got %d", expected, result)
    }
}
```

Run tests with:

sh
CopyEdit
```
go test
```

---

we covered:

■ Go's basic syntax (packages, functions, variables, loops, and conditionals)
■ How to write, compile, and run Go programs
■ Go's development workflow (formatting, dependency management, and testing)

With this foundation, you're now ready to start **building more complex programs!** 🚀

Running Go Programs from the Terminal

Now that you're familiar with Go's syntax and workflow, let's explore how to **run Go programs** directly from the terminal. Unlike some interpreted languages like Python, Go is a **compiled language**, meaning the code needs to be processed into an executable file before running. However, Go also provides a quick way to execute code without manually compiling it every time.

Using go run to Execute Go Programs

If you just want to **run a Go program without compiling it separately**, use the go run command. This command compiles and runs your Go code **in one step**.

Example: Running a Go file directly

1. Open your terminal or command prompt.

Navigate to the directory where your Go file is located.
sh
CopyEdit

```
cd path/to/your/project
```

2. Run the program with:
   sh
   CopyEdit

   ```
   go run main.go
   ```

Example Output

CopyEdit

Hello, Go!

■ **Pros of go run:**

- Quick execution for development and testing.
- No need to generate an executable file manually.

✘ **Cons of go run:**

- Slightly slower because it compiles the program every time before running.
- Not ideal for distributing compiled programs.

Compiling Go Programs with go build

If you need to generate an **executable binary** that can be run without Go installed, use go build. This compiles the Go program into an independent file.

Example: Compiling a Go Program

sh

CopyEdit

go build main.go

This creates an **executable file** in the same directory:

- On **Linux/macOS**, it will be named main.
- On **Windows**, it will be named main.exe.

To run the compiled program, execute:

sh

CopyEdit

```
./main    # On Linux/macOS

main.exe  # On Windows
```

■ **Pros of** go build:

- The program runs faster since it doesn't need to recompile every time.
- You can **share the binary** with others, even if they don't have Go installed.

✗ **Cons of** go build:

- Takes up more storage than go run.
- Requires an extra step compared to go run.

Cross-Compiling for Different Operating Systems

Go makes it easy to **compile programs for different platforms** without needing the actual system.

Example: Compiling for Windows on a Linux/macOS Machine

sh

CopyEdit

```
GOOS=windows GOARCH=amd64 go build -o myprogram.exe main.go
```

Example: Compiling for macOS on Windows/Linux

sh

CopyEdit

```
GOOS=darwin GOARCH=amd64 go build -o myprogram main.go
```

Example: Compiling for Linux on macOS/Windows

sh

CopyEdit

```
GOOS=linux GOARCH=amd64 go build -o myprogram main.go
```

This allows you to **build Go programs for different operating systems** without needing multiple machines.

Your First Go Program: "Hello, World!"

Now that you understand how to run Go programs, let's officially write our **first Go program**—the famous **"Hello, World!"** example. This simple program prints a message to the console and introduces key concepts of Go.

Step 1: Create a New Go File

Navigate to your Go workspace and create a new file named hello.go:

sh

CopyEdit

touch hello.go

Or use a text editor like VS Code, Vim, or Notepad++ to create the file.

Step 2: Write the "Hello, World!" Program

Open hello.go and enter the following code:

go

CopyEdit

```
package main

import "fmt"

func main() {
    fmt.Println("Hello, World!")
}
```

Step 3: Run the Program

To execute the program, open your terminal and navigate to the directory containing hello.go. Then run:

sh

CopyEdit

```
go run hello.go
```

■ Expected Output:

CopyEdit

```
Hello, World!
```

Breaking Down the Code

Let's analyze the components of our first Go program:

1. package main

go

CopyEdit

```
package main
```

- Every Go program must belong to a **package**.
- The main package is **required for executables**.

2. Importing a Package

go

CopyEdit

```
import "fmt"
```

- We use the fmt package (short for **format**) to handle **printing text to the console**.
- The import statement allows us to use functions from the **standard library**.

3. The main Function

go

CopyEdit

```
func main() {

    fmt.Println("Hello, World!")

}
```

- The main() function is **where execution begins**.
- The fmt.Println function **prints text to the console** followed by a **newline**.
- The **double quotes** ("") indicate a string in Go.

46

Variations of "Hello, World!" in Go

①Using fmt.Print Instead of fmt.Println

go

CopyEdit

```
fmt.Print("Hello, World!")
```

Difference:

- Print does **not add a newline** at the end.
- The output will appear on the same line with any following print statements.

---

②Using a Variable for the Message

go

CopyEdit

```
message := "Hello, World!"

fmt.Println(message)
```

Why use this?

- This makes the code **more flexible**, allowing you to change the message easily.

---

3 Using a Function to Print the Message

go

CopyEdit

```go
func sayHello() {

    fmt.Println("Hello, World!")

}

func main() {

    sayHello()

}
```

Why use this?

- Functions allow **code reuse** and **cleaner organization**.

Common Errors When Running Your First Go Program

✗ Forgetting the package main Declaration

If you don't include package main, Go won't know this is an executable program.

✗ Misspelling fmt.Println

Go **does not allow unused or misspelled imports**, so this will throw an error.

✗ Using Single Quotes for Strings

Go **uses double quotes ("") for strings**, not single quotes (''), which are for characters.

48

Congratulations! 🎉 You have:

✔ Learned how to **run Go programs** using go run and go build

✔ Written your first Go program: **"Hello, World!"**

✔ Understood **Go's package system, imports, and functions**

✔ Learned about **common mistakes and best practices**

In the next section, we'll dive into **variables, data types, and operators in Go**, so you can start writing more dynamic programs! 🚀

Understanding the Go Toolchain

The Go toolchain is a **set of built-in tools** that help developers write, build, test, and manage Go programs. Unlike many other programming languages that require external build systems or package managers, Go provides an **all-in-one toolchain** to handle everything.

Go's toolchain includes:

■ **go run** – Runs a Go program without compiling a binary.

■ **go build** – Compiles a Go program into an executable binary.

■ **go install** – Installs a compiled Go program to the system's GOPATH.

■ **go mod** – Manages dependencies using Go Modules.

■ **go test** – Runs tests for Go programs.

■ **go fmt** – Formats Go code according to Go's style guide.

■ **go vet** – Detects potential issues in Go code.

■ **go doc** – Displays documentation for Go packages.

Let's go through the most commonly used tools in Go's toolchain.

1. Running Go Programs with go run

As we covered earlier, go run allows you to quickly execute a Go program without creating an executable.

Example:

sh

CopyEdit

```
go run main.go
```

This is useful for **testing and debugging** small programs but isn't ideal for production since it recompiles the code every time.

---

2. Compiling and Building with go build

When you're ready to create a **standalone executable**, use go build.

Example:

sh

CopyEdit

```
go build main.go
```

This creates a **compiled binary** (main or main.exe on Windows), which you can run without Go installed.

If your project contains multiple files, simply run go build in the project directory:

sh

CopyEdit

go build

This builds the entire project into a single executable.

■ **Why use go build?**

- Produces a **standalone binary**.
- Ideal for **production deployment**.

---

3. Installing Programs with go install

If you want to **install a Go program system-wide**, use go install. This compiles and places the binary in Go's bin directory, making it accessible globally.

Example:

sh

CopyEdit

go install github.com/example/mytool

Now, you can run mytool from anywhere in your terminal.

■ **Why use** go install?

- Useful for **command-line tools**.
- Installs programs globally for easy access.

---

4. Managing Dependencies with go mod

Modern Go uses **Go Modules** to manage dependencies. If your project relies on external libraries, Go Modules handle them automatically.

Initialize a Go Module in a New Project

sh

CopyEdit

go mod init my-go-project

This creates a go.mod file, which tracks dependencies.

Adding Dependencies

To install a package, use:

sh

CopyEdit

go get github.com/gorilla/mux

This updates go.mod and go.sum (which keeps track of package versions).

■ Why use Go Modules?

- No need to set up a GOPATH.
- Dependencies are **self-contained in the project**.

---

5. Testing Code with go test

Go includes a built-in testing framework. You can write tests in _test.go files and run them with:

sh

CopyEdit

```
go test
```

Example test:

go

CopyEdit

```
package main

import "testing"

func TestAdd(t *testing.T) {

    result := Add(2, 3)

    if result != 5 {
```

```
t.Errorf("Expected 5 but got %d", result)

    }

}
```

Why use go test?

- Ensures code **works as expected**.
- Helps maintain code **reliability**.

---

6. Checking Code with go vet

Before running your Go program, it's a good idea to **check for common mistakes** using go vet:

sh

CopyEdit

go vet main.go

Why use go vet?

- Detects **potential bugs and logic errors**.
- Helps catch **misused variables and functions**.

---

7. Viewing Documentation with go doc

If you need help with a Go package, go doc provides **built-in documentation**.

Example: Viewing documentation for fmt

sh

CopyEdit

```
go doc fmt
```

To view documentation for a specific function:

sh

CopyEdit

```
go doc fmt.Println
```

■ **Why use go doc?**

- Quickly access **official documentation** without searching online.

Formatting Code with gofmt

Go has a **strict coding style**, and instead of debating code formatting, Go enforces a consistent style using gofmt. This **automatically formats** your Go code according to Go's official style guide.

Why Use gofmt?

■ Ensures **consistent code style** across teams.

■ Removes **extra spaces, incorrect indentation, and messy formatting**.

■ Helps avoid **style disagreements**.

Using gofmt to Format Go Code

To format a single Go file:

sh

CopyEdit

```
gofmt -w main.go
```

- The -w flag **writes changes directly to the file**.

To format all Go files in a directory:

sh

CopyEdit

```
gofmt -w .
```

Before and After gofmt

Before Formatting (Messy Code)

go

CopyEdit

```go
package main

import "fmt"

func main() {fmt.Println("Hello, Go!") }
```

After Running gofmt

go

CopyEdit

```go
package main

import "fmt"


func main() {

    fmt.Println("Hello, Go!")

}
```

Notice how gofmt:

- **Fixed indentation**.
- **Separated import statements**.
- **Properly structured the function body**.

Checking Formatting Without Modifying the File

If you just want to **check** formatting without changing the file, use:

sh

CopyEdit

```
gofmt -d main.go
```

This displays the **differences** between the current and properly formatted versions.

Automatically Formatting Code on Save (VS Code Setup)

If you're using **VS Code**, you can set Go code to **format automatically on save**:

1. Open VS Code settings.
2. Search for "editor.formatOnSave" and enable it.
3. Install the **Go extension** for auto-formatting.

■ Now, every time you save a file, gofmt **will format it automatically!**

In this section, we covered:

■ **The Go toolchain** – Essential Go commands like go run, go build, go test, and go mod.

■ **Dependency management** – How Go Modules handle packages.

■ **Code formatting with** gofmt – Ensuring Go code follows best practices.

Go's built-in tools **simplify development** and ensure consistency. In the next chapter, we'll dive into **variables, data types, and operators** so you can start writing more complex programs! 🚀

Chapter 3: Go Fundamentals – Variables, Data Types, and Operators

Understanding **variables and data types** is one of the most important steps in learning Go. In this chapter, we'll cover **how to declare variables**, explore **Go's primitive data types**, and discuss **best practices for working with data**.

Declaring Variables in Go

What is a Variable?

A variable is a **storage location** in memory that holds a value. In Go, variables must be **declared before use**, and their types are determined at compile time.

---

1. Declaring Variables Using the var Keyword

The most traditional way to declare a variable in Go is by using the var keyword.

Basic Syntax:

go

CopyEdit

```
var variableName type = value
```

Example: Declaring Variables with var

go

CopyEdit

```go
package main

import "fmt"

func main() {
    var name string = "Alice"
    var age int = 25
    var height float64 = 5.6
    var isStudent bool = false

    fmt.Println(name, age, height, isStudent)
}
```

Output:

arduino

CopyEdit

```
Alice 25 5.6 false
```

---

2. Declaring Variables Without an Initial Value

If you don't assign a value, Go automatically assigns a **default zero value** based on the data type.

Example: Default Zero Values

go

CopyEdit

```
var message string  // Default: ""
var count int       // Default: 0
var temperature float64  // Default: 0.0
var isActive bool   // Default: false
```

■ **Best practice:** Always initialize variables if you know their values in advance.

---

3. Using Short Variable Declaration (:=)

Go provides a **shortcut** for declaring and initializing variables using :=. This is called **short variable declaration**.

Example: Using := for Quick Assignments

go

CopyEdit

```
name := "Bob"   // Go automatically detects type as string
age := 30       // Type inferred as int
height := 6.1   // Type inferred as float64
isEmployed := true  // Type inferred as bool

fmt.Println(name, age, height, isEmployed)
```

Key points:

✔ := automatically infers the data type.

✔ Works only **inside functions** (not at the package level).

✔ Cannot be used if a variable is already declared.

---

4. Declaring Multiple Variables at Once

You can **declare multiple variables** in one line to keep code clean.

Example: Group Declaration

go

CopyEdit

```
var (
    firstName string = "John"
    lastName  string = "Doe"
    age       int    = 28
    salary    float64 = 50000.00
)
```

This is useful when declaring **related variables** together.

---

5. Constant Variables (const)

In Go, you can declare **constants** using const. Constants **cannot be changed** after they are assigned.

Example: Declaring Constants

go

CopyEdit

```
const pi = 3.14159
```

```go
const appName = "Go Fundamentals"
```

🚀 **Use constants for values that never change, like mathematical values or configuration settings.**

Primitive Data Types in Go

Go provides several **primitive data types** that are commonly used in programs. These include **strings, integers, floating-point numbers, and booleans**.

---

1. Strings (string)

A string is a **sequence of characters** enclosed in double quotes ("").

Example: Working with Strings

go
CopyEdit
```go
var greeting string = "Hello, Go!"
fmt.Println(greeting)
```

Concatenating Strings

go
CopyEdit
```go
firstName := "Alice"
lastName := "Johnson"
fullName := firstName + " " + lastName
```

```go
fmt.Println(fullName) // Output: Alice Johnson
```

Getting the Length of a String

go
CopyEdit
```go
message := "Hello, World!"
fmt.Println(len(message)) // Output: 13
```

Accessing Individual Characters

go
CopyEdit
```go
word := "GoLang"
fmt.Println(string(word[0])) // Output: G
```

(Note: Strings in Go are **immutable**—you cannot change characters directly.)

---

2. Integers (int)

Go provides several types of integers based on **size and sign**.

Type	Size	Range
int8	8 bits	-128 to 127
int16	16 bits	-32,768 to 32,767
int32	32 bits	-2,147,483,648 to 2,147,483,647
int64	64 bits	-9 quintillion to 9 quintillion
int	Depends on OS (32-bit or 64-bit)	

🚀 Best Practice:

- Use int unless you need a specific size (int8, int16, etc.).
- Use uint (unsigned int) if the value **will never be negative**.

Example: Declaring Integers

go
CopyEdit

```
var age int = 30
var population int64 = 8000000000
fmt.Println(age, population)
```

---

3. Floating-Point Numbers (float32, float64)

Floating-point numbers represent **decimal values**.

Type	Size	Precision
float32	32 bits	6-7 decimal digits
float64	64 bits	15-16 decimal digits

Example: Working with Floats

go
CopyEdit

```
var price float64 = 99.99
var temperature float32 = 36.6
fmt.Println(price, temperature)
```

- ◆ **Best Practice:** Always use float64 unless memory constraints require float32.

---

4. Boolean (bool)

A boolean holds **true** or **false** values.

Example: Boolean Variables

go

CopyEdit

```
var isRunning bool = true
fmt.Println(isRunning)  // Output: true
```

Boolean Logic with Conditionals

go

CopyEdit

```
isWeekend := true
if isWeekend {
    fmt.Println("Relax, it's the weekend!")
} else {
    fmt.Println("Time to work!")
}
```

Key Takeaways

✔ **Go is statically typed**, meaning variable types are fixed at compile time.

✔ Use var for explicit declarations and := for inferred types inside functions.

✔ **Primitive data types** include **strings, integers, floats, and booleans**.

✔ Strings are **immutable**, and integers come in **various sizes**.

✔ Floating-point numbers require **float32 or float64**, with float64 being the default.

✔ Boolean values are either **true or false** and are useful for logic operations.

Constants and Type Inference

In Go, constants are **fixed values** that do not change throughout the execution of a program. They are useful for defining values like **mathematical constants, configuration values, or fixed parameters** that remain the same.

Declaring Constants

Constants are defined using the const keyword. Unlike variables, constants **must be assigned a value at the time of declaration.**

Example: Basic Constant Declaration

go

CopyEdit

```
package main

import "fmt"

const pi float64 = 3.14159

const appName = "Go Fundamentals" // Type inferred as string
```

```go
func main() {

    fmt.Println("Pi:", pi)

    fmt.Println("Application:", appName)

}
```

Output:

makefile

CopyEdit

Pi: 3.14159

Application: Go Fundamentals

Constant Expressions and Arithmetic

Constants can be used in **expressions**.

go

CopyEdit

const width = 10

const height = 5

69

```go
const area = width * height

func main() {

    fmt.Println("Area:", area)

}
```

Output:

makefile

CopyEdit

Area: 50

- **Key points about constants in Go:**

✔ Cannot be changed after declaration.

✔ Must be **assigned a value immediately**.

✔ Can be **used in arithmetic operations**.

Type Inference in Go

Go allows **implicit type inference**, meaning it can **automatically determine the type** based on the assigned value.

Example: Type Inference

go

CopyEdit

```go
func main() {

    x := 42  // Automatically inferred as int

    y := 3.14 // Automatically inferred as float64

    message := "Hello, Go!"  // Inferred as string


    fmt.Println(x, y, message)

}
```

✔ **Benefits of Type Inference:**

- Reduces **code verbosity**.
- Allows **quicker variable declarations**.
- Makes code **cleaner and easier to read**.

Operators in Go

Operators allow you to perform **mathematical calculations, logical comparisons, and bitwise operations**. Go supports **arithmetic, logical, relational, and bitwise operators**.

1. Arithmetic Operators

Arithmetic operators perform **basic math operations**.

Operator	Description	Example
+	Addition	x + y
-	Subtraction	x - y
*	Multiplication	x * y
/	Division	x / y
%	Modulus (remainder)	x % y

Example: Arithmetic Operations

go

CopyEdit

```go
func main() {

    a := 10

    b := 3


    fmt.Println("Addition:", a + b)      // 13

    fmt.Println("Subtraction:", a - b)   // 7

    fmt.Println("Multiplication:", a * b) // 30

    fmt.Println("Division:", a / b)      // 3 (integer division)
```

```go
fmt.Println("Modulus:", a % b)        // 1
}
```

✔ **Note:** Integer division in Go **discards decimal values**. To get precise results, convert integers to floats.

go

CopyEdit

```go
fmt.Println("Division (float):", float64(a) / float64(b))  // 3.3333
```

---

2. Comparison Operators

Comparison operators **compare two values** and return a boolean result (true or false).

Operator	Description	Example
==	Equal to	x == y
!=	Not equal to	x != y
>	Greater than	x > y
<	Less than	x < y
>=	Greater than or equal to	x >= y
<=	Less than or equal to	x <= y

Example: Using Comparison Operators

go

CopyEdit

```go
func main() {
```

```
x := 10

y := 20

fmt.Println(x == y) // false

fmt.Println(x != y) // true

fmt.Println(x > y)  // false

fmt.Println(x < y)  // true

}
```

---

3. Logical Operators

Logical operators are used in **Boolean expressions**.

Operator	Description	Example
&&	Logical AND	x > 5 && y < 10
`		
!	Logical NOT	!true (false)

Example: Logical Operators

go

CopyEdit

```
func main() {

    a := true

    b := false
```

```go
fmt.Println(a && b)  // false

fmt.Println(a || b)  // true

fmt.Println(!a)      // false
}
```

---

4. Bitwise Operators

Bitwise operators work at the **binary level**, manipulating bits directly.

Operator	Description	Example
&	Bitwise AND	x & y
`	`	Bitwise OR
^	Bitwise XOR	x ^ y
<<	Left shift	x << 2
>>	Right shift	x >> 2

Example: Bitwise Operations

go

CopyEdit

```go
func main() {

    x := 5  // Binary: 0101

    y := 3  // Binary: 0011
```

```go
fmt.Println(x & y)  // 1 (0001)

fmt.Println(x | y)  // 7 (0111)

fmt.Println(x ^ y)  // 6 (0110)

fmt.Println(x << 1) // 10 (1010)

fmt.Println(x >> 1) // 2 (0010)

}
```

🚀 **Bitwise operations are useful in cryptography, graphics, and performance optimization.**

Type Conversion and Best Practices

Go is a **statically typed language**, meaning **you cannot mix different data types in an operation** without **explicit conversion**.

---

1. Type Conversion in Go

Use **type conversion functions** to convert between types.

Example: Converting Integers and Floats

go

```go
func main() {
    var x int = 10
    var y float64 = 3.5

    sum := float64(x) + y
    fmt.Println(sum) // 13.5
}
```

Example: Converting Strings to Integers

go

```go
import "strconv"

func main() {
    str := "42"
    num, _ := strconv.Atoi(str) // Convert string to int
    fmt.Println(num + 10) // 52
}
```

🚀 **Best Practice:** Always check for errors when converting strings.

---

2. Best Practices for Using Variables and Operators

◼ Use := for short declarations inside functions

go

CopyEdit

```
age := 25  // Instead of: var age int = 25
```

◼ Use meaningful variable names

go

CopyEdit

```
userAge := 30  // Instead of: x := 30
```

◼ Be mindful of integer division

go

CopyEdit

```
fmt.Println(10 / 3)  // 3 (not 3.33)
```

Convert to float for accurate division:

go

CopyEdit

```
fmt.Println(float64(10) / 3)  // 3.3333
```

■ **Avoid unnecessary type conversions**

go

CopyEdit

```
// BAD: Unnecessary conversion
var x float64 = float64(42)
```

■ **Use constants where values should not change**

go

CopyEdit

```
const pi = 3.14159
```

✔ **Constants** are fixed values that **cannot change**.
✔ **Go automatically infers types** when using :=.

✔ **Operators** allow arithmetic, logical, and bitwise calculations.

✔ **Type conversion** is required when working with mixed types.

In the next section, we'll explore **control structures like loops and conditionals** to build more dynamic programs! 🚀

Chapter 4: Control Flow in Go – Loops and Conditionals

Control flow determines the **logical flow** of a program. In Go, we use **conditional statements** (if, else, switch) and **loops** (for) to **execute code based on conditions or repetitions**. This chapter will cover **how to make decisions in Go programs** using if statements, the switch statement, and their practical applications.

Using if, else if, and else Statements

Conditional statements allow programs to make **decisions** based on certain conditions.

---

1. Basic if Statement

The if statement **executes a block of code only if a condition is true**.

Syntax:

```go
CopyEdit
if condition {
    // Code executes if condition is true
}
```

Example: Checking a Single Condition

go

CopyEdit

```
package main

import "fmt"

func main() {
    age := 18

    if age >= 18 {
        fmt.Println("You are eligible to vote.")
    }
}
```

Output:

css

CopyEdit

```
You are eligible to vote.
```

If age was 17, the program would print nothing because the condition age >= 18 would be **false**.

---

2. Using else for Alternative Cases

An else block runs when the if condition is **false**.

go

CopyEdit

```
if condition {
    // Executes if condition is true
} else {
    // Executes if condition is false
}
```

Example: Handling Two Conditions

go
CopyEdit

```
func main() {
    temperature := 15

    if temperature > 20 {
        fmt.Println("It's warm outside.")
    } else {
        fmt.Println("It's cold outside.")
    }
}
```

Output:

rust
CopyEdit

```
It's cold outside.
```

3. Using else if for Multiple Conditions

If you have **multiple conditions**, you can use else if.

go

CopyEdit

```
if condition1 {
    // Executes if condition1 is true
} else if condition2 {
    // Executes if condition2 is true
} else {
    // Executes if neither condition1 nor condition2 is true
}
```

Example: Categorizing Scores

go

CopyEdit

```
func main() {
    score := 85

    if score >= 90 {
        fmt.Println("Grade: A")
    } else if score >= 80 {
        fmt.Println("Grade: B")
    } else if score >= 70 {
        fmt.Println("Grade: C")
    } else {
        fmt.Println("Grade: F")
    }
```

}

Output:

makefile
CopyEdit
Grade: B

---

4. Declaring Variables Inside if Statements

You can declare a variable **directly inside an if statement**.

Example: Short Variable Declaration Inside if

go
CopyEdit

```go
if num := 10; num%2 == 0 {
    fmt.Println("Even number")
} else {
    fmt.Println("Odd number")
}
```

Output:

typescript
CopyEdit
Even number

Here, num is **scoped** to the if-else block and does not exist outside it.

---

5. Checking Multiple Conditions with Logical Operators

You can use **logical operators** ($\&\&$, ||, !) inside conditions.

Example: Checking Multiple Conditions

go

CopyEdit

```go
func main() {
    age := 22
    hasID := true

    if age >= 18 && hasID {
        fmt.Println("Allowed to enter the club.")
    } else {
        fmt.Println("Access denied.")
    }
}
```

Output:

css

CopyEdit

```
Allowed to enter the club.
```

✔ $\&\&$ (AND) ensures **both conditions** are true.

✔ || (OR) checks if **at least one condition** is true.

The switch Statement and Its Benefits

The switch statement is an **alternative to multiple if-else if conditions**. It simplifies code when **checking a variable against multiple values**.

---

1. Basic switch Statement

Instead of writing multiple if-else conditions, switch allows **cleaner and more readable code**.

Example: Using switch to Evaluate a Single Variable

go
CopyEdit

```
package main

import "fmt"

func main() {
    day := "Monday"

    switch day {
    case "Monday":
        fmt.Println("Start of the workweek!")
    case "Friday":
        fmt.Println("Weekend is near!")
    case "Saturday", "Sunday":
        fmt.Println("It's the weekend!")
    default:
        fmt.Println("A regular weekday.")
```

```
    }
}
```

Output:

sql

CopyEdit

Start of the workweek!

✔ case **labels** check against specific values.

✔ **Multiple values can be handled in one** case (e.g., "Saturday", "Sunday").

✔ default **runs when no other case matches**.

---

2. The switch Statement with Expressions

You can also evaluate **expressions** instead of just values.

Example: Categorizing Numbers

go

CopyEdit

```
func main() {
    number := 15

    switch {
    case number < 10:
        fmt.Println("The number is small.")
    case number >= 10 && number < 20:
        fmt.Println("The number is medium.")
```

```go
    default:
        fmt.Println("The number is large.")
    }
}
```

Output:

csharp
CopyEdit
The number is medium.

🚀 **Key benefits of this approach:**

- No need to write switch variable at the start.
- More flexible than standard switch statements.

---

3. Using fallthrough in a switch Statement

By default, once a case matches, Go **does not check further cases**. However, you can use fallthrough to **continue execution to the next case**.

Example: Using fallthrough

go
CopyEdit
```go
func main() {
    rating := 4

    switch rating {
```

```go
case 5:
    fmt.Println("Excellent!")
    fallthrough
case 4:
    fmt.Println("Great job!")
case 3:
    fmt.Println("Good effort!")
default:
    fmt.Println("Needs improvement.")
    }
}
```

Output:

CopyEdit

Great job!
Good effort!

✔ fallthrough allows execution to continue to the **next case** even if it does not match.

---

4. The switch Statement with interface{} (Dynamic Types)

Go's switch statement can be used with **different data types**.

Example: Checking Different Types

go
CopyEdit

```go
func checkType(i interface{}) {
    switch v := i.(type) {
```

```go
        case int:
            fmt.Println("Integer:", v)
        case string:
            fmt.Println("String:", v)
        case bool:
            fmt.Println("Boolean:", v)
        default:
            fmt.Println("Unknown type")
    }
}

func main() {
    checkType(42)
    checkType("hello")
    checkType(true)
}
```

Output:

vbnet
CopyEdit
Integer: 42
String: hello
Boolean: true

✔ interface{} is a **generic type** that can hold any value.
✔ .(type) is used for **type assertion** inside the switch statement.

✔ Use if, else if, and else for **decision-making**.

✔ Declare variables **inside** if for cleaner code.

✔ Use switch for **simpler and cleaner** condition handling.

✔ fallthrough allows cases to **continue executing**.

✔ switch can handle **expressions and different data types**.

Loops are an essential part of programming, allowing us to **execute code repeatedly**. Unlike many other languages that have multiple loop structures (such as for, while, and do-while), Go **only has one looping construct**: the for loop. This keeps the language simple and efficient while still providing the flexibility to perform a wide range of iterations.

Looping with for: The Only Loop You Need in Go

In Go, the for loop is used to **iterate over sequences, perform repeated actions, and automate tasks**.

---

1. Basic for Loop

The most common form of a for loop includes **initialization, condition, and increment**.

Syntax:

go

CopyEdit

```
for initialization; condition; increment {

    // Code to execute in each iteration
```

}

Example: Counting from 1 to 5

go

CopyEdit

```go
package main

import "fmt"

func main() {
    for i := 1; i <= 5; i++ {
        fmt.Println("Iteration:", i)
    }
}
```

Output:

makefile

CopyEdit

```
Iteration: 1
```

Iteration: 2

Iteration: 3

Iteration: 4

Iteration: 5

- ◆ **Breakdown:**

  - i := 1 → Initialize the loop variable i.
  - i <= 5 → Loop continues **while i is less than or equal to 5**.
  - i++ → Increments i by 1 after each iteration.

---

2. Using for as a while Loop

Go doesn't have a separate while loop, but you can **mimic it using for**.

Example: Looping Until a Condition is Met

go

CopyEdit

```
func main() {
    count := 0


    for count < 5 { // Acts like a while loop
```

```
    fmt.Println("Count:", count)

    count++

  }

}
```

Output:

makefile

CopyEdit

Count: 0

Count: 1

Count: 2

Count: 3

Count: 4

✔ This loop continues **as long as** count < 5.

---

3. Infinite for Loop

A for loop without a condition runs **forever** until manually stopped.

Example: Creating an Infinite Loop

go

CopyEdit

```go
func main() {
    for {
        fmt.Println("This will run forever!")
    }
}
```

🔋 **Warning:** Infinite loops **must be manually terminated** using break or return, or by stopping the program (Ctrl + C in terminal).

---

4. Looping Over Collections (Slices and Maps)

Go's for loop can be used with **range** to iterate over arrays, slices, and maps.

Example: Looping Over a Slice

go

CopyEdit

```go
func main() {
    numbers := []int{10, 20, 30, 40, 50}
```

```go
for index, value := range numbers {

    fmt.Println("Index:", index, "Value:", value)

}

}
```

Output:

diff

CopyEdit

Index: 0 Value: 10

Index: 1 Value: 20

Index: 2 Value: 30

Index: 3 Value: 40

Index: 4 Value: 50

✔ index gives the position, and value holds the **element at that index**.

---

5. Iterating Over Maps

When working with **maps**, range returns **key-value pairs**.

Example: Looping Over a Map

go

CopyEdit

```go
func main() {
    person := map[string]int{"Alice": 30, "Bob": 25, "Charlie": 35}

    for name, age := range person {
        fmt.Println(name, "is", age, "years old.")
    }
}
```

Output:

csharp

CopyEdit

```
Alice is 30 years old.

Bob is 25 years old.

Charlie is 35 years old.
```

✔ This is **useful for working with dictionaries and JSON data.**

98

Breaking and Continuing Loops

In Go, break and continue provide extra control over loops.

---

1. Stopping a Loop with break

The break statement **exits a loop immediately**.

Example: Breaking a Loop When a Condition is Met

go

CopyEdit

```go
func main() {

  for i := 1; i <= 10; i++ {

    if i == 5 {

      fmt.Println("Breaking the loop at:", i)

      break

    }

    fmt.Println("Iteration:", i)

  }

}
```

Output:

vbnet

CopyEdit

Iteration: 1

Iteration: 2

Iteration: 3

Iteration: 4

Breaking the loop at: 5

✔ The loop **stops at** i == 5 instead of running until 10.

---

2. Skipping an Iteration with continue

The continue statement **skips the current iteration and moves to the next one**.

Example: Skipping Even Numbers

go

CopyEdit

```
func main() {
    for i := 1; i <= 10; i++ {
```

```go
    if i%2 == 0 {

        continue // Skip even numbers

    }

    fmt.Println("Odd number:", i)

    }

}
```

Output:

yaml

CopyEdit

Odd number: 1

Odd number: 3

Odd number: 5

Odd number: 7

Odd number: 9

✔ The loop **skips even numbers** using continue.

_____

3. Using break in an Infinite Loop

A common use case is **stopping an infinite loop with break**.

Example: Breaking an Infinite Loop

go

CopyEdit

```go
func main() {
    i := 0

    for {
        if i == 3 {
            fmt.Println("Stopping at:", i)
            break
        }
        fmt.Println("Running iteration:", i)
        i++
    }
}
```

Output:

yaml

CopyEdit

Running iteration: 0

Running iteration: 1

Running iteration: 2

Stopping at: 3

✔ **Always use break in infinite loops** to prevent endless execution.

Common Pitfalls and Best Practices

🔔 Pitfall 1: Forgetting the Loop Condition (Infinite Loops)

go

CopyEdit

```
for { // No condition
    fmt.Println("Oops! This runs forever.")
}
```

✔ **Best Practice:** Always ensure a way to **exit** the loop.

🪨 **Pitfall 2: Modifying a Slice While Iterating**

go

CopyEdit

```
numbers := []int{1, 2, 3}

for i, val := range numbers {

    numbers = append(numbers, val*2) // Modifying inside loop

}
```

✖ This can cause **unexpected behavior or infinite loops**.

✔ **Best Practice:** Avoid modifying slices **while iterating** over them.

🪨 **Pitfall 3: Forgetting to Use continue Properly**

go

CopyEdit

```
for i := 1; i <= 5; i++ {

    continue

    fmt.Println(i) // This will NEVER execute
```

}

✔ **Best Practice:** Place continue **before** the code you want to skip.

🪨 **Pitfall 4: Using == Instead of := in Loop Conditions**

go

CopyEdit

for i == 0; i < 5; i++ { // ✖ Wrong

✔ **Best Practice:** Use := for variable declarations (i := 0).

✔ **Go uses only for loops**, replacing while and do-while.
✔ **for loops can iterate over slices, maps, and strings** using range.
✔ **Use break to exit loops early** and continue to **skip an iteration**.
✔ **Infinite loops must be manually terminated** to avoid program freezes.
✔ **Avoid modifying slices while iterating over them** to prevent unexpected behavior.

Chapter 5: Functions and Error Handling in Go

Functions are the **building blocks** of Go programs, allowing us to write reusable and organized code. In this chapter, we'll cover how to **define functions, pass parameters, return multiple values, and use variadic functions**.

Defining Functions: Syntax and Parameters

A **function** is a block of code that performs a **specific task**. Functions help **avoid repetition**, improve **code readability**, and make debugging easier.

---

1. Basic Function Syntax

A function in Go is declared using the func keyword, followed by the **function name, parameters (optional), and return type (optional)**.

Syntax:

go
CopyEdit

```
func functionName(parameters) returnType {
    // Function body
    return value  // Optional
}
```

---

2. Example: Simple Function Without Parameters

go
CopyEdit

```go
package main

import "fmt"

func greet() {
   fmt.Println("Hello, Go!")
}

func main() {
   greet() // Calling the function
}
```

Output:

CopyEdit
```
Hello, Go!
```

✔ This function **does not accept parameters** and **does not return a value**.

---

3. Function with Parameters

Functions can take **parameters** to accept input values.

Example: Function with Parameters

go

CopyEdit

```
func add(a int, b int) int {
    return a + b
}

func main() {
    sum := add(5, 3)
    fmt.Println("Sum:", sum)
}
```

Output:

makefile
CopyEdit

Sum: 8

✔ The function **accepts two integers (a and b) and returns an integer**.

🚀 **Best Practice:**

- Always **use descriptive parameter names** to improve readability.

---

4. Multiple Parameters with the Same Type

If multiple parameters have the **same type**, you can declare the type only once.

Example: Declaring Parameter Type Once

go
CopyEdit

```go
func multiply(x, y int) int {
    return x * y
}

func main() {
    result := multiply(4, 5)
    fmt.Println("Product:", result)
}
```

Output:

makefile
CopyEdit
Product: 20

✔ This syntax makes function definitions **cleaner**.

---

5. Functions Without a Return Value

Some functions **perform actions but don't return a value**.

Example: Function That Prints a Message
go
CopyEdit
```go
func sayHello(name string) {
    fmt.Println("Hello,", name)
}
```

```
func main() {
    sayHello("Alice")
}
```

Output:

CopyEdit

```
Hello, Alice
```

✔ **No return statement needed** since the function simply prints a message.

Returning Multiple Values in Go

Unlike many other languages, Go allows **functions to return multiple values**. This is useful when a function needs to return **more than one piece of data**.

---

1. Example: Returning Multiple Values

go

CopyEdit

```
func divide(a, b int) (int, int) {
    quotient := a / b
    remainder := a % b
    return quotient, remainder
}

func main() {
```

```go
    q, r := divide(10, 3)
    fmt.Println("Quotient:", q, "Remainder:", r)
}
```

Output:

makefile
CopyEdit

Quotient: 3 Remainder: 1

✔ This function **returns both the quotient and remainder**.

---

2. Ignoring a Return Value

If you don't need one of the returned values, use _ (underscore) to ignore it.

go
CopyEdit

```go
func main() {
    q, _ := divide(10, 3) // Ignoring remainder
    fmt.Println("Quotient:", q)
}
```

✔ This avoids **unused variable warnings**.

---

3. Named Return Values

You can **name return values** inside the function signature. This makes code more readable.

go
CopyEdit

```
func calculate(a, b int) (sum int, product int) {
    sum = a + b
    product = a * b
    return
}

func main() {
    s, p := calculate(4, 5)
    fmt.Println("Sum:", s, "Product:", p)
}
```

✔ Named return values **automatically return assigned values**.

Variadic Functions and Their Use Cases

A **variadic function** allows passing a **variable number of arguments**. This is useful when you **don't know in advance how many values will be provided**.

---

1. Declaring a Variadic Function

A variadic function **uses ... before the parameter type**.

Example: Function That Accepts Multiple Arguments

go

CopyEdit

```
func sum(numbers ...int) int {
    total := 0
    for _, num := range numbers {
        total += num
    }
    return total
}

func main() {
    result := sum(1, 2, 3, 4, 5)
    fmt.Println("Sum:", result)
}
```

Output:

makefile

CopyEdit

```
Sum: 15
```

✔ numbers ...int allows passing **any number of integers**.

---

2. Passing a Slice to a Variadic Function

You can **pass a slice** to a variadic function using ... after the slice.

Example: Passing a Slice

go

CopyEdit

```
func main() {
    nums := []int{2, 4, 6, 8, 10}
    result := sum(nums...) // Expanding the slice
    fmt.Println("Sum:", result)
}
```

Output:

makefile

CopyEdit

```
Sum: 30
```

✔ nums... **expands the slice** into individual arguments.

---

3. Mixing Regular and Variadic Parameters

Variadic parameters must **always be the last parameter** in the function.

Example: Regular and Variadic Parameters

go

CopyEdit

```
func greetUsers(prefix string, names ...string) {
```

```go
    for _, name := range names {
        fmt.Println(prefix, name)
    }
}

func main() {
    greetUsers("Hello,", "Alice", "Bob", "Charlie")
}
```

Output:

CopyEdit

```
Hello, Alice
Hello, Bob
Hello, Charlie
```

✔ prefix is a **regular parameter**, and names ...string allows multiple values.

✔ **Functions in Go are defined using func and can return multiple values.**

✔ **Use := to store function return values when calling a function.**

✔ **Go supports named return values, which improves readability.**

✔ **Variadic functions allow functions to accept a variable number of arguments.**

✔ **Use _ to ignore unwanted return values from a function.**

Anonymous Functions and Closures

Go allows defining functions without names, known as anonymous functions. These functions are useful for short-lived logic, inline function execution, and closures.

---

1. Declaring an Anonymous Function

An anonymous function does not have a name and can be assigned to a variable.

Example: Assigning an Anonymous Function to a Variable

go

CopyEdit

```go
package main

import "fmt"

func main() {
    add := func(a, b int) int {
        return a + b
    }
```

```go
    result := add(3, 7)

    fmt.Println("Sum:", result)

}
```

Output:

makefile

CopyEdit

Sum: 10

✔ **The function is declared and stored in a variable (add), which can be used like any regular function.**

---

2. Immediately Invoking an Anonymous Function

An anonymous function can be executed immediately after defining it.

Example: Self-Executing Anonymous Function

go

CopyEdit

```go
func main() {

    result := func(a, b int) int {
```

```
    return a * b

}(4, 5)


    fmt.Println("Product:", result)

}
```

Output:

makefile

CopyEdit

```
Product: 20
```

✔ **This function does not need a separate function call.**
✔ **The parameters** $(4, 5)$ **are passed immediately after defining the function.**

---

3. Closures: Functions That Capture Variables

A closure is an anonymous function that retains access to variables from its surrounding scope.

Example: Closure That Retains State

go

CopyEdit

```go
func counter() func() int {

    count := 0

    return func() int {

        count++ // Retains value of count

        return count

    }

}


func main() {

    nextCount := counter()


    fmt.Println(nextCount()) // 1

    fmt.Println(nextCount()) // 2

    fmt.Println(nextCount()) // 3

}
```

Output:

CopyEdit

1

2

3

✔ The counter function returns an anonymous function, which remembers (captures) the count variable even after counter() has finished executing.

🚀 Use cases of closures:

- Maintaining state across function calls.
- Encapsulating logic without exposing variables.

Understanding and Handling Errors in Go

Unlike many languages that use try-catch blocks for error handling, Go explicitly handles errors using return values.

---

1. The Standard Go Error Handling Pattern

In Go, functions return an error as the last return value.

Example: Returning an Error

go

CopyEdit

```go
package main

import (
    "errors"
    "fmt"
)

func divide(a, b int) (int, error) {
    if b == 0 {
        return 0, errors.New("division by zero is not allowed")
    }
    return a / b, nil
}

func main() {
    result, err := divide(10, 0)
```

```
if err != nil {

    fmt.Println("Error:", err)

} else {

    fmt.Println("Result:", result)

}

}
```

Output:

vbnet

CopyEdit

Error: division by zero is not allowed

✔ errors.New("message") **creates a new error.**
✔ **The function returns** (int, error), **handling both success and failure cases.**
✔ nil **means no error occurred.**

---

2. Checking for Errors Properly

Always check for errors after calling a function that returns an error.

Example: Error Handling in File Operations

go

CopyEdit

```go
package main

import (
    "fmt"
    "os"
)

func main() {
    file, err := os.Open("nonexistent.txt")

    if err != nil {
        fmt.Println("Error:", err)
        return
    }

    fmt.Println("File opened successfully:", file.Name())
```

```
}
```

Output:

perl

CopyEdit

Error: open nonexistent.txt: no such file or directory

✔ **If an error occurs, handle it gracefully instead of letting the program crash.**

---

3. Returning Custom Errors

Go allows creating and returning custom error messages.

Example: Custom Error Function

go

CopyEdit

```go
package main

import (

    "errors"

    "fmt"
```

```go
)


func validateAge(age int) error {

    if age < 18 {

        return errors.New("age must be 18 or older")

    }

    return nil

}


func main() {

    err := validateAge(16)


    if err != nil {

        fmt.Println("Validation failed:", err)

    } else {

        fmt.Println("Validation passed")

    }

}
```

Output:

yaml

CopyEdit

Validation failed: age must be 18 or older

✔ errors.New() is used to create a custom error message.
✔ The function returns nil if there is no error.

The errors Package: Creating Custom Errors

The errors package provides tools for creating and handling errors more effectively.

---

1. Using fmt.Errorf for Detailed Errors

The fmt.Errorf function allows formatting error messages dynamically.

Example: Creating a Custom Error Message

go

CopyEdit

```
package main

import (

    "fmt"
```

```go
)


func divide(a, b int) (int, error) {

    if b == 0 {

        return 0, fmt.Errorf("cannot divide %d by zero", a)

    }

    return a / b, nil

}


func main() {

    result, err := divide(15, 0)


    if err != nil {

        fmt.Println("Error:", err)

    } else {

        fmt.Println("Result:", result)

    }

}
```

Output:

vbnet

CopyEdit

Error: cannot divide 15 by zero

✔ fmt.Errorf() **formats the error message dynamically.**

---

2. Wrapping Errors Using errors.Join

From Go 1.20, the errors.Join() function allows combining multiple errors into one.

Example: Combining Multiple Errors

go

CopyEdit

```
package main

import (

    "errors"

    "fmt"

)

func process() error {

    err1 := errors.New("database connection failed")
```

```go
    err2 := errors.New("cache service not responding")

    return errors.Join(err1, err2)
}

func main() {
    err := process()

    if err != nil {
        fmt.Println("Errors:", err)
    }
}
```

Output:

css

CopyEdit

Errors: database connection failed; cache service not responding

✔ **This is useful when handling multiple failures in a single function.**

3. Using errors.Is to Compare Errors

Sometimes, you need to check if an error matches a specific type.

Example: Checking for a Specific Error

go

CopyEdit

```go
package main

import (

    "errors"

    "fmt"

)


var ErrNotFound = errors.New("resource not found")


func getResource(id int) error {

    if id == 0 {

        return ErrNotFound

    }
```

```go
    return nil

}


func main() {

    err := getResource(0)


    if errors.Is(err, ErrNotFound) {

        fmt.Println("Resource not found!")

    }

}
```

Output:

CopyEdit

Resource not found!

✔ errors.Is() **checks if an error matches a predefined error constant.**

✔ **Anonymous functions allow defining functions without names.**
✔ **Closures retain access to variables from the surrounding scope.**

✔ Errors are returned explicitly instead of using exceptions.

✔ Use errors.New() and fmt.Errorf() to create meaningful error messages.

✔ Use errors.Join() to combine multiple errors in Go 1.20+.

✔ Check for specific errors using errors.Is().

Chapter 6: Structs and Interfaces: Object-Oriented Programming in Go

Understanding Structs and Methods

Go is not an object-oriented programming (OOP) language in the traditional sense like Java or C++, but it **supports object-oriented principles** in a unique way. At the core of Go's OOP-like features are **structs** and **methods**. These allow you to group related data and define behaviors for those data types.

1. What Are Structs?

A **struct** is a composite data type in Go that groups variables (called fields) together. Unlike arrays or slices, which can store multiple values of the same type, a **struct** can hold multiple fields of **different types**.

Example: Defining a Struct

go
CopyEdit

```
package main

import "fmt"

// Define a struct for a Car
type Car struct {
```

```go
    Brand string
    Model string
    Year  int
}

func main() {
    // Initialize the struct
    myCar := Car{
        Brand: "Tesla",
        Model: "Model S",
        Year:  2022,
    }

    fmt.Println("Car Details:", myCar)
}
```

Output:

css
CopyEdit
Car Details: {Tesla Model S 2022}

✔ **Structs are simple** and are ideal for representing complex data types that involve **multiple attributes**.

✔ Each **field** in the struct can be of a **different type**, making structs versatile for many real-world applications.

---

2. Defining Methods on Structs

In Go, we can define **methods on structs** by specifying a **receiver**. The receiver is a variable that represents the struct instance in the method.

Example: Adding Methods to a Struct

go

CopyEdit

```go
package main

import "fmt"

// Define the struct
type Car struct {
    Brand string
    Model string
    Year  int
}

// Method with receiver `c` of type `Car`
func (c Car) GetCarInfo() string {
    return fmt.Sprintf("%d %s %s", c.Year, c.Brand, c.Model)
}

func main() {
    myCar := Car{
        Brand: "Tesla",
        Model: "Model S",
        Year:  2022,
    }
```

```go
// Call the method
fmt.Println(myCar.GetCarInfo())
}
```

Output:

yaml
CopyEdit
2022 Tesla Model S

✔ The method GetCarInfo is defined for the Car struct and takes the **instance of the struct** (c in this case) as a receiver.
✔ Methods allow **defining behaviors** that relate to the data within the struct.

---

3. Pointer Receivers vs Value Receivers

When defining methods, Go allows you to choose between **pointer receivers** and **value receivers**.

- **Value receivers** work on a **copy** of the struct.
- **Pointer receivers** work on the **actual struct**, allowing changes to the original data.

Example: Pointer Receiver

go
CopyEdit
package main

```go
import "fmt"

// Define the struct
type Car struct {
    Brand string
    Model string
    Year  int
}

// Method with pointer receiver
func (c *Car) UpdateYear(newYear int) {
    c.Year = newYear
}

func main() {
    myCar := Car{
        Brand: "Tesla",
        Model: "Model S",
        Year:  2022,
    }

    fmt.Println("Before:", myCar)
    myCar.UpdateYear(2023)
    fmt.Println("After:", myCar)
}
```

Output:

yaml

CopyEdit

Before: {Tesla Model S 2022}
After: {Tesla Model S 2023}

✔ Using a **pointer receiver** allows you to **modify the original struct** instance directly.

✔ When you need to modify the struct's fields, prefer **pointer receivers**.

Struct Composition and Embedding

Go allows **struct composition** through **embedding**. Struct embedding allows one struct to be nested within another, enabling reuse and promoting a form of **inheritance-like behavior**.

---

1. What is Struct Embedding?

Embedding a struct in another struct essentially **inherits** the fields and methods of the embedded struct. This is similar to **inheritance** in OOP, but with **a more flexible approach**.

Example: Struct Embedding

go

CopyEdit

```
package main
```

138

```go
import "fmt"

// Define the Engine struct
type Engine struct {
    Horsepower int
}

// Method for Engine
func (e Engine) Start() {
    fmt.Println("Engine started with", e.Horsepower, "horsepower.")
}

// Define the Car struct which embeds Engine
type Car struct {
    Brand  string
    Model  string
    Engine // Embedded struct
}

func main() {
    myCar := Car{
        Brand:  "Tesla",
        Model:  "Model S",
        Engine: Engine{Horsepower: 1020},
    }

    fmt.Println("Car Details:", myCar)
    myCar.Start() // Calling method from the embedded Engine struct
}
```

Output:

yaml
CopyEdit
Car Details: {Tesla Model S {1020}}
Engine started with 1020 horsepower.

✔ **Struct embedding** allows the Car struct to **inherit the Start method** from the Engine struct.
✔ Go's composition-based model is **flexible** and doesn't rely on rigid inheritance.

---

2. Promoting Methods via Embedding

Methods defined on the embedded struct can be **automatically promoted** to the outer struct. This means the outer struct can **access the embedded struct's methods** as though they were its own.

Example: Promoting Methods
go
CopyEdit
```
package main

import "fmt"

type Engine struct {
    Horsepower int
}
```

```go
func (e Engine) Start() {
    fmt.Println("Engine started with", e.Horsepower, "horsepower.")
}

type Car struct {
    Brand  string
    Model  string
    Engine // Embedding Engine struct
}

func main() {
    myCar := Car{
        Brand:  "Tesla",
        Model:  "Model S",
        Engine: Engine{Horsepower: 1020},
    }

    fmt.Println("Car Info:", myCar)
    myCar.Start() // Calling Engine's Start method directly on Car
}
```

Output:

yaml
CopyEdit
Car Info: {Tesla Model S {1020}}
Engine started with 1020 horsepower.

✔ The method Start() from the Engine struct is **directly callable on the Car struct** due to **method promotion**.

✔ **Struct composition** in Go is a powerful tool that **simplifies inheritance** and makes your code **more modular**.

---

3. Using Embedding for Reusable Components

Struct embedding can be an effective way to **reuse components** in a more **modular** way. This allows your code to stay **dry** (Don't Repeat Yourself) by **separating concerns** into different structs and embedding them where needed.

Example: Reusable Components

go
CopyEdit

```
package main

import "fmt"

// Define structs for Engine and Transmission
type Engine struct {
    Horsepower int
}

func (e Engine) Start() {
    fmt.Println("Engine started with", e.Horsepower, "horsepower.")
}

type Transmission struct {
    Type string
```

142

```go
    }

    func (t Transmission) Shift() {
        fmt.Println("Shifting to", t.Type, "transmission.")
    }

    // Define Car struct that embeds Engine and Transmission
    type Car struct {
        Brand        string
        Model        string
        Engine       // Embedded struct
        Transmission // Embedded struct
    }

    func main() {
        myCar := Car{
            Brand:  "Tesla",
            Model:  "Model S",
            Engine: Engine{Horsepower: 1020},
            Transmission: Transmission{Type: "Automatic"},
        }

        fmt.Println("Car Info:", myCar)
        myCar.Start()
        myCar.Shift()
    }
```

Output:

yaml

CopyEdit

Car Info: {Tesla Model S {1020} {Automatic}}
Engine started with 1020 horsepower.
Shifting to Automatic transmission.

✔ In this example, we've made **Engine** and **Transmission** reusable components by embedding them into the Car struct.

✔ This allows for **easy extension** and **modular design** of your application.

- **Structs** allow you to group multiple fields of different types to represent complex data.
- You can define **methods on structs**, enabling behaviors related to the data.
- Go supports **pointer receivers** for modifying the original struct and **value receivers** for working with copies of the struct.
- **Struct composition** (embedding) is a powerful feature that promotes **code reuse** and enables an inheritance-like behavior.
- You can **promote methods from embedded structs**, making it easy to reuse functionality across your program.
- Struct embedding is a **flexible, modular way** to organize your code and build complex systems.

Defining and Using Interfaces

What Is an Interface in Go?

An **interface** in Go is a **type** that specifies a set of **method signatures**. If a struct implements all the methods in an interface, it is said to **satisfy** that interface. Importantly, Go's interfaces are **implicit**—you don't need to explicitly declare that a type implements an interface. If it has the methods, it implements the interface.

Key Characteristics of Interfaces in Go:

- An interface defines behavior without specifying how it is implemented.
- A type satisfies an interface if it **implements all the methods** required by the interface.
- You don't explicitly declare that a type implements an interface. It's done automatically.

Defining an Interface

An interface can be defined using the type keyword followed by the interface name and method signatures.

Example: Defining an Interface

go

CopyEdit

package main

```go
import "fmt"

// Define the Speaker interface
type Speaker interface {

    Speak() string

}

// Define a struct
type Person struct {

    Name string

}

// Implement the Speak method for the Person struct
func (p Person) Speak() string {

    return "Hello, my name is " + p.Name

}

func main() {
```

```go
    // Create an instance of Person
    p := Person{Name: "Alice"}


    // Use the Speak method defined in the Speaker interface
    var s Speaker = p
    fmt.Println(s.Speak()) // Output: Hello, my name is Alice
}
```

Output:

csharp

CopyEdit

Hello, my name is Alice

In the above example:

- The Speaker interface defines a Speak() method.
- The Person struct implements this method, which makes it satisfy the Speaker interface.
- You can store an instance of Person in a variable of type Speaker and call the Speak() method.

Empty Interface

Go also has an **empty interface**, which is defined as:

go

CopyEdit

```
type Interface interface{}
```

The empty interface can hold values of any type because it has no methods. It's often used for **generic programming** or when you need to work with data of unknown type.

Using Interfaces in Practice

Interfaces are incredibly powerful for **decoupling** and **polymorphism** in Go. They allow you to define **general behaviors** that can be implemented by any type, providing flexibility in your programs.

Example: Using Interfaces for Polymorphism

go

CopyEdit

```
package main

import "fmt"
```

```go
// Define the Shape interface

type Shape interface {

    Area() float64

}


// Define the Circle struct

type Circle struct {

    Radius float64

}


// Define the Rectangle struct

type Rectangle struct {

    Length, Width float64

}


// Implement the Area method for Circle

func (c Circle) Area() float64 {

    return 3.14 * c.Radius * c.Radius

}
```

```go
// Implement the Area method for Rectangle

func (r Rectangle) Area() float64 {

    return r.Length * r.Width

}



// Function that takes a Shape interface as an argument

func printArea(s Shape) {

    fmt.Println("Area:", s.Area())

}



func main() {

    // Create instances of Circle and Rectangle

    c := Circle{Radius: 5}

    r := Rectangle{Length: 4, Width: 6}



    // Pass both types to the printArea function

    printArea(c) // Output: Area: 78.5

    printArea(r) // Output: Area: 24
```

}

Output:

makefile

CopyEdit

Area: 78.5

Area: 24

In this example:

- Both Circle and Rectangle types implement the Shape interface by defining the Area() method.
- The printArea function can accept any type that satisfies the Shape interface, allowing it to work with **different types** in a **polymorphic manner**.

Interfaces vs. Structs: When to Use Each

In Go, **structs** and **interfaces** are two fundamental concepts that are used to model data and behavior, but they serve different purposes. Here's a comparison to help you decide when to use each.

1. Use Structs When:

- **Storing Data:** Structs are ideal for grouping **related fields** together to represent a **single entity**.
- **Defining Data Types:** Use structs to define **complex types** with attributes that need to be stored together, like Car, Person, or Product.
- **Representing Real-World Objects:** Structs are often used when you need to represent concrete **real-world entities** that have **specific attributes**.

Example: Using Structs

go

CopyEdit

```
type Car struct {

    Brand string

    Model string

    Year  int

}
```

A Car struct is used when you want to store information about a specific car. Each Car has a Brand, Model, and Year.

2. Use Interfaces When:

- **Defining Behaviors:** Interfaces are best used when you want to define **abstract behaviors** that can be implemented by different types. They are ideal when different types need to **perform the same action** but may implement it differently.

- **Decoupling Components:** Interfaces allow you to write **decoupled code** where the functionality of one part of the system is independent of other parts.
- **Polymorphism:** Interfaces enable **polymorphism**, allowing you to work with different types of objects in a generic way, such as a collection of objects that all satisfy the same interface.

Example: Using Interfaces for Polymorphism

go

CopyEdit

```
type Shape interface {

    Area() float64

}
```

The Shape interface is used to define behavior that can be implemented by different types (e.g., Circle, Rectangle, etc.). The interface allows you to work with any shape that implements the Area() method.

---

3. Structs and Interfaces Together

In many Go programs, structs and interfaces are used together. You can define structs to hold data and implement interfaces to define behavior for that data.

Example: Combining Structs and Interfaces

go

CopyEdit

```go
type Animal interface {
    Speak() string
}


type Dog struct {
    Name string
}


func (d Dog) Speak() string {
    return d.Name + " says Woof!"
}


type Cat struct {
    Name string
}
```

```go
func (c Cat) Speak() string {

    return c.Name + " says Meow!"

}


func main() {

    var animal Animal

    dog := Dog{Name: "Buddy"}

    cat := Cat{Name: "Whiskers"}


    animal = dog

    fmt.Println(animal.Speak()) // Output: Buddy says Woof!


    animal = cat

    fmt.Println(animal.Speak()) // Output: Whiskers says Meow!

}
```

In this example:

- We define the Animal interface with a Speak() method.

- The Dog and Cat structs implement this method, so they satisfy the Animal interface.
- This allows us to work with both Dog and Cat types using the **same interface**.

- **Interfaces** define behavior in Go and allow types to **implement behaviors** without needing to explicitly declare them.
- Go's interfaces are **implicitly satisfied**, meaning any type with the right methods automatically satisfies the interface.
- **Structs** are used for storing **data**, while **interfaces** are used for defining **abstract behaviors** that can be implemented by different types.
- Interfaces enable **polymorphism**, allowing you to treat different types in a **generic way** if they implement the same methods.
- Combining **structs** and **interfaces** allows for a **modular, flexible design**, where you can define data structures and their behaviors separately.

Implementing Polymorphism in Go

What Is Polymorphism in Go?

Polymorphism, in the context of programming, refers to the ability of different types to be treated as instances of the same type through inheritance, interfaces, or both. In Go, **polymorphism** is primarily achieved through **interfaces**, allowing you to define behaviors that can be shared by multiple types.

How Go Achieves Polymorphism

In Go, polymorphism is accomplished when multiple types implement the same interface. This allows you to write functions or methods that can work with **any type** that satisfies the interface, without knowing the concrete type ahead of time.

Go's polymorphism is **implicit**, meaning that you don't need to explicitly declare a type's implementation of an interface. As long as a type has the methods required by an interface, it automatically implements the interface.

The Key Advantage of Polymorphism in Go

The primary advantage of polymorphism is **decoupling**. It allows you to write functions or methods that work with different types, as long as they satisfy the interface. This is particularly useful in scenarios where you need to interact with different types that share common behaviors but don't need to know about their internal structure.

Example: Polymorphism in Action

Let's consider a **vehicle management system** where we have different types of vehicles, such as **Car** and **Bike**. Both of these types can implement a common Vehicle interface with a Drive() method.

Step 1: Define the Interface

go

CopyEdit

```
package main
```

```go
import "fmt"
```

```go
// Vehicle interface defines a common behavior (Drive)
type Vehicle interface {

    Drive() string

}
```

Step 2: Implement the Interface with Structs

Now, we define two structs, Car and Bike, both of which implement the Drive() method.

go

CopyEdit

```go
// Car struct
type Car struct {

    Make  string

    Model string

}


// Implement the Drive method for Car
func (c Car) Drive() string {
```

```go
    return "Driving a " + c.Make + " " + c.Model

}


// Bike struct

type Bike struct {

    Make  string

    Type  string

}


// Implement the Drive method for Bike

func (b Bike) Drive() string {

    return "Riding a " + b.Make + " " + b.Type + " bike"

}
```

Step 3: Using Polymorphism

We can now write a function that works with any type that satisfies the Vehicle interface.

go

CopyEdit

```go
// Function that accepts the Vehicle interface
```

```go
func StartVehicle(v Vehicle) {

    fmt.Println(v.Drive())

}


func main() {

    // Create instances of Car and Bike

    car := Car{Make: "Toyota", Model: "Corolla"}

    bike := Bike{Make: "Yamaha", Type: "Mountain"}


    // Use polymorphism to handle different types

    StartVehicle(car) // Output: Driving a Toyota Corolla

    StartVehicle(bike) // Output: Riding a Yamaha Mountain bike

}
```

Output:

css

CopyEdit

Driving a Toyota Corolla

Riding a Yamaha Mountain bike

In this example:

- The Vehicle interface defines a Drive() method.
- Both Car and Bike types implement the Drive() method, so they satisfy the Vehicle interface.
- The StartVehicle() function can work with any type that implements Drive(), which demonstrates **polymorphism** in Go.

Practical Examples: Building a Simple User Management System

Now that you understand how polymorphism works in Go, let's apply it in a more practical scenario. In this section, we will build a **simple user management system** using Go's polymorphic features.

The Problem:

You need to manage different types of users in a system: **Admin** users and **Regular** users. Each user type should have the ability to perform common actions, such as **logging in**, **viewing a dashboard**, and **performing tasks**. However, admins should have additional privileges, such as accessing the **admin dashboard** and **performing administrative tasks**.

Step 1: Define the User Interface

We begin by defining a common interface User that includes methods common to all types of users.

go

```go
package main

import "fmt"

// User interface defines the common behaviors
type User interface {
    Login() string
    ViewDashboard() string
}
```

Step 2: Define the Admin and Regular User Structs

Next, we define two types of users: **Admin** and **RegularUser**. Both types will implement the User interface, but **Admin** will have additional functionality.

go

```go
// Admin struct represents an administrator
type Admin struct {
    Name string
```

```go
}


// RegularUser struct represents a regular user

type RegularUser struct {

    Name string

}


// Admin implements the Login method

func (a Admin) Login() string {

    return a.Name + " has logged in as an Admin."

}


// Admin implements the ViewDashboard method

func (a Admin) ViewDashboard() string {

    return "Viewing the Admin Dashboard."

}


// RegularUser implements the Login method

func (r RegularUser) Login() string {
```

```go
    return r.Name + " has logged in as a Regular User."

}

// RegularUser implements the ViewDashboard method

func (r RegularUser) ViewDashboard() string {

    return "Viewing the Regular User Dashboard."

}

// Admin-specific method

func (a Admin) PerformAdminTask() string {

    return a.Name + " is performing an admin task."

}
```

Step 3: Write the Function to Interact with Users

We write a function to interact with any user, regardless of whether they are an admin or a regular user. This function will demonstrate **polymorphism** by using the User interface.

go

CopyEdit

```go
// Function to manage user login and dashboard view

func ManageUser(u User) {

    fmt.Println(u.Login())
```

```go
	fmt.Println(u.ViewDashboard())

}

func main() {

	// Create instances of Admin and RegularUser

	admin := Admin{Name: "Alice"}

	regular := RegularUser{Name: "Bob"}

	// Use polymorphism to manage users

	ManageUser(admin)   // Output: Alice has logged in as an Admin. Viewing the Admin Dashboard.

	ManageUser(regular) // Output: Bob has logged in as a Regular User. Viewing the Regular User Dashboard.

	// Admin-specific task

	fmt.Println(admin.PerformAdminTask()) // Output: Alice is performing an admin task.

}
```

Output:

csharp

CopyEdit

Alice has logged in as an Admin.

Viewing the Admin Dashboard.

Bob has logged in as a Regular User.

Viewing the Regular User Dashboard.

Alice is performing an admin task.

In this example:

- The User interface defines the common behaviors (Login() and ViewDashboard()).
- Both the Admin and RegularUser types implement these behaviors, so we can call them using the User interface.
- The Admin type has an additional method, PerformAdminTask(), that only admins can perform.
- This demonstrates how polymorphism allows us to handle both user types generically while still providing the ability to call specific methods when needed.

Extending the System: Adding More User Roles

If we wanted to extend the user management system to support additional user roles, like **Guest** users or **Moderator** users, we could do so without changing the existing code for the User interface or the ManageUser function. You would simply create new types that implement the User interface and define their specific behavior.

- **Polymorphism** in Go is achieved through interfaces, which allow you to define shared behavior across different types.

- Go's **implicit interfaces** make polymorphism straightforward and flexible, as you don't need to explicitly declare that a type implements an interface.
- Polymorphism enables **decoupling** and **flexibility** in your code, allowing you to write more generic functions and methods that work with any type that satisfies the interface.
- The **user management system** example demonstrates how to use interfaces and polymorphism to handle different types of users, each with specific behaviors.

Chapter 7: Working with Packages and Modules in Go

What Are Go Packages?

In Go, **packages** are a fundamental part of how code is organized. They allow you to structure your application in a modular way, making it easier to maintain and share. A **package** is simply a collection of Go source files that are grouped together under a common directory. Each package can contain one or more files, but all files within a package must belong to the same directory.

The Purpose of Packages

Packages serve several important purposes in Go:

1. **Code Reusability**: Packages allow you to write code once and reuse it across multiple parts of your program.
2. **Modularity**: By grouping related functions, types, and methods into separate packages, you can break your program into smaller, manageable pieces.
3. **Organization**: Packages make your code easier to navigate and understand. It allows you to logically separate different parts of your application (such as database access, user authentication, and network communication).

In Go, the **standard library** is a set of packages that are included with Go and provide common functionality like file I/O, networking, and string manipulation. You can also create your own custom packages to organize your code.

Basic Structure of a Go Package

Each Go package typically includes:

- A **Go source file** that contains functions, variables, constants, and types.
- A **package** **statement** at the top of each Go file to define the package name.

Let's look at a basic example of how a package is structured.

Step 1: Creating a Custom Package

Suppose you want to create a package called mathutils that contains utility functions for mathematical operations like addition and subtraction.

Here's how you can organize your code:

go
CopyEdit

```go
// mathutils/mathutils.go
package mathutils

// Add function to add two integers
func Add(a int, b int) int {
    return a + b
}

// Subtract function to subtract b from a
func Subtract(a int, b int) int {
    return a - b
}
```

In this example:

- The file mathutils.go is part of the mathutils package.
- It contains two functions: Add and Subtract.

Step 2: Using Your Package

Now that you have created the mathutils package, you can use it in your main program or other packages. Here's how:

go

CopyEdit

```go
// main.go
package main

import (
    "fmt"
    "path/to/your/project/mathutils" // Import the mathutils package
)

func main() {
    sum := mathutils.Add(5, 3)
    difference := mathutils.Subtract(8, 4)

    fmt.Println("Sum:", sum)              // Output: Sum: 8
    fmt.Println("Difference:", difference) // Output: Difference: 4
}
```

In this example:

- We import the mathutils package using the import keyword and the path to the package.
- We then call the Add and Subtract functions from the mathutils package.

Package Visibility

In Go, the **visibility** of functions, variables, and types is determined by their **naming convention**:

- **Uppercase names** (e.g., Add, Subtract) are **exported**, meaning they are accessible from other packages.
- **Lowercase names** (e.g., add, subtract) are **unexported**, meaning they are private to the package and cannot be accessed from outside.

Understanding Go Modules (go mod init)

What Are Go Modules?

Go Modules are a feature introduced in Go 1.11 to manage dependencies and package versions. Before Go Modules, managing dependencies in Go was done using **GOPATH**. However, this approach had several limitations, particularly with managing multiple versions of dependencies and keeping code isolated. Go Modules allow developers to manage dependencies more effectively, making it easier to handle external packages and libraries in a way that works across different environments.

A **Go module** is a collection of Go packages that are tracked together, with a module-level version that is used to manage dependencies. Go Modules use the go.mod file to record the module name and its dependencies.

Benefits of Go Modules

1. **Versioning**: Go Modules provide the ability to specify which version of a dependency your project uses.

2. **Isolation**: Each project is self-contained, which prevents version conflicts between different projects.

3. **Compatibility**: You no longer need to worry about the GOPATH, as modules can exist outside of the GOPATH directory.

4. **Reproducible Builds**: By using a go.mod file, you can ensure that your project uses the exact same versions of dependencies every time you build your application.

Setting Up a Go Module: go mod init

To start using Go Modules in your project, you need to initialize a Go module by running the go mod init command. This will create a go.mod file that tracks the dependencies for your project.

Step 1: Initialize the Go Module

Navigate to the root directory of your project and run the following command:

bash
CopyEdit

```
go mod init example.com/myproject
```

In this example:

- example.com/myproject is the **module path**, which is typically the path to your repository. If you're working locally, you can use any name for the module path, but for public repositories, this should match the repository's URL.

This will create a go.mod file in your project's root directory, which might look something like this:

go
CopyEdit
```
module example.com/myproject

go 1.17
```

The go.mod file contains:

- The **module path** (your project's import path).
- The **Go version** you're using in your project.

Step 2: Add Dependencies

To add dependencies to your project, simply import them into your code. For example, if you want to use a third-party package like github.com/gorilla/mux (a router for HTTP requests), you can import it as you normally would:

go
CopyEdit
```
package main

import (
    "fmt"
```

```go
    "github.com/gorilla/mux"
)

func main() {
    r := mux.NewRouter()
    fmt.Println(r)
}
```

Once you add this import, run the following command:

bash
CopyEdit
```
go mod tidy
```

This command will:

- Download the required dependencies.
- Add the dependencies to your go.mod file.
- Create or update a go.sum file, which ensures the integrity of the downloaded dependencies.

The go.mod file will now include something like this:

go
CopyEdit
```
module example.com/myproject

go 1.17

require github.com/gorilla/mux v1.8.0
```

Step 3: Work with Dependencies

Now that your module is initialized and dependencies are added, you can start building your Go project and managing the dependencies using Go's module system. You don't need to worry about **GOPATH** anymore, as Go will handle downloading and managing your dependencies automatically.

To see all the dependencies and their versions for your project, you can run:

bash
CopyEdit
```
go list -m all
```

This will list all the dependencies in your project, including transitive dependencies (dependencies of your dependencies).

Upgrading and Removing Dependencies

To upgrade a dependency to a newer version, you can run:

bash
CopyEdit
```
go get github.com/gorilla/mux@latest
```

To remove an unused dependency, you can simply delete the import statement from your code and then run:

bash
CopyEdit
```
go mod tidy
```

This will remove any dependencies that are no longer being used in the project.

Best Practices for Working with Go Modules

1. **Keep Your go.mod File Clean**: Use go mod tidy regularly to clean up unnecessary dependencies and keep your module up to date.
2. **Use Semantic Versioning**: When managing dependencies, prefer using versions that follow **semantic versioning** (e.g., v1.0.0, v1.2.0).
3. **Pin Your Dependencies**: Ensure you use fixed versions of dependencies to avoid unexpected changes when newer versions are released.
4. **Avoid Using replace Unless Necessary**: The replace directive in the go.mod file can be useful for testing, but should be avoided in production code, as it can break reproducibility.
5. **Use Go Proxy**: By default, Go fetches modules from the Go Proxy (proxy.golang.org), which ensures fast and secure fetching of dependencies.

- **Packages** in Go are used to organize and reuse code across your project.
- You can create custom packages to group related functions and types together, which promotes modularity and clean code.
- **Go Modules** make dependency management easy by eliminating the need for GOPATH, providing versioning, and ensuring reproducible builds.
- The go mod init command initializes a Go module, which generates a go.mod file to track dependencies.
- Go Modules allow you to manage dependencies easily, adding, upgrading, and removing them with simple commands.

Importing and Using Third-Party Packages

One of the most powerful features of Go is its ability to easily import and use third-party packages from the Go ecosystem, which allows you to leverage functionality already created by others. These packages can help you add complex features to your application without having to reinvent the wheel.

Why Use Third-Party Packages?

Using third-party packages is essential for productivity and efficiency in Go development. These packages save you time, provide robust solutions to common problems, and integrate easily with your existing code. Common uses for third-party packages include:

- Handling HTTP requests and routing (e.g., gorilla/mux)
- Managing data storage (e.g., gorm for ORM functionality)
- Working with JSON or XML data (e.g., jsoniter for faster JSON parsing)
- Implementing security features (e.g., bcrypt for password hashing)

Go makes it incredibly simple to use third-party libraries, thanks to its built-in tooling with Go Modules.

How to Import Third-Party Packages

To import a third-party package, you'll need to use the **import statement** and include the path to the package repository. Here's an example of importing a popular HTTP router package called gorilla/mux.

Step 1: Install the Package

To use a third-party package, first, install it by running the go get command:

bash

CopyEdit

go get github.com/gorilla/mux

This command does the following:

- Downloads the package from the specified repository.
- Adds the package to your go.mod file as a dependency.

Step 2: Import and Use the Package

Once the package is installed, you can import it into your Go code and use its functions and types. Here's an example:

go

CopyEdit

```
package main

import (

    "fmt"

    "github.com/gorilla/mux" // Import the third-party package

    "net/http"

)
```

```go
func main() {

    // Create a new router

    r := mux.NewRouter()

    // Define routes and handlers

    r.HandleFunc("/", func(w http.ResponseWriter, r *http.Request) {

        fmt.Fprintf(w, "Hello, world!")

    })

    // Start the server

    http.ListenAndServe(":8080", r)

}
```

In this example:

- We imported the mux package from the github.com/gorilla/mux path.
- We then created a new router using mux.NewRouter() and added a simple route.
- Finally, we used http.ListenAndServe to start the server and pass in our router.

Step 3: Manage the Package in Your Project

Once you've added a third-party package to your code, Go will track it in the go.mod file, where the version of the package will be stored. The go.mod file ensures that you are using the correct version of the package every time you build your project.

To check the current status of your dependencies, run:

bash

CopyEdit

```
go list -m all
```

This will display a list of all the dependencies, including third-party packages, in your project.

Updating Third-Party Packages

If you want to update a third-party package to its latest version, you can use the following command:

bash

CopyEdit

```
go get github.com/gorilla/mux@latest
```

This updates the mux package to the latest version, as recorded in your go.mod file.

If you want to update all dependencies at once, you can use:

bash

CopyEdit

```
go get -u
```

This command will update all your dependencies to the latest minor or patch versions, based on the constraints in the go.mod file.

Creating and Using Your Own Packages

In Go, creating and using your own packages is straightforward. Structuring your project into packages not only improves code organization, but it also enhances maintainability and reusability. Creating your own packages follows the same principles as importing third-party packages, but instead of pulling code from external repositories, you define your own functionality.

Why Create Your Own Packages?

1. **Modularity**: You can separate different parts of your code into distinct, logical units, making it easier to manage and understand.
2. **Reusability**: Once you create a package, it can be reused in different parts of your application or even across multiple projects.
3. **Maintainability**: By isolating complex logic into separate packages, you can make future updates and bug fixes easier.

How to Create a Go Package

To create your own package in Go, simply create a new directory for the package and put one or more Go source files in it. The directory name will become the name of your package.

Step 1: Create a Package Directory

For example, let's create a package called mathutils to handle basic mathematical operations.

1. Create a new directory for the package, for example: mathutils.
2. Inside that directory, create a Go file (e.g., mathutils.go):

go

CopyEdit

```go
// mathutils/mathutils.go

package mathutils

// Add function adds two integers

func Add(a, b int) int {

    return a + b

}

// Multiply function multiplies two integers

func Multiply(a, b int) int {

    return a * b

}
```

In this example:

- We've created a mathutils package in a new directory.
- The mathutils.go file contains two functions: Add and Multiply.

Step 2: Import and Use Your Custom Package

Once your package is created, you can import and use it in other parts of your project. Here's how to do that:

1. Navigate to the directory where your main program resides (e.g., main.go).
2. Import your custom package just like you would import a third-party package.

go

CopyEdit

```go
// main.go

package main

import (

    "fmt"

    "path/to/your/project/mathutils" // Import your custom package

)

func main() {

    result1 := mathutils.Add(5, 7)

    result2 := mathutils.Multiply(4, 6)

        fmt.Println("Sum:", result1)      // Output: Sum: 12

        fmt.Println("Product:", result2)   // Output: Product: 24

}
```

In this example:

- We imported our custom mathutils package by providing its path relative to the main.go file.
- We used the Add and Multiply functions from the mathutils package.

Step 3: Package Visibility

Just like third-party packages, the visibility of functions, variables, and types in your own packages is determined by their naming convention:

- **Uppercase names** (e.g., Add, Multiply) are **exported** and can be accessed from other packages.
- **Lowercase names** (e.g., add, multiply) are **unexported** and can only be accessed within the same package.

Best Practices for Creating and Using Packages

1. **Organize by Functionality**: Group related functions together into one package. For example, put all mathematical functions in a mathutils package and all file-related operations in a fileutils package.
2. **Use Descriptive Names**: Name your packages and functions based on their functionality to make your code self-documenting.
3. **Keep Functions Small**: Each function should do one thing and do it well. This improves the readability and maintainability of your packages.
4. **Avoid Circular Dependencies**: Ensure that packages do not depend on each other in a circular fashion, as this can lead to complex, hard-to-debug issues.
5. **Export Only What's Needed**: Don't export every function or variable in your package. Export only what is necessary for other packages to use.

- **Third-party packages** in Go can be easily imported and used to add functionality to your project. Go Modules handle the management of dependencies seamlessly.
- When working with third-party packages, you can install, import, and update them effortlessly, thanks to the Go Modules system.

- **Creating your own packages** is simple and follows the same principles as importing third-party packages. Organizing your code into packages promotes modularity and reusability.
- Go encourages good practices when it comes to **package visibility** and code organization. Be mindful of naming conventions and maintain a clean, modular structure.

Best Practices for Code Organization and Managing Dependencies with go get

In any programming language, good code organization is critical to the maintainability, readability, and scalability of a project. Go, with its simplicity and strict conventions, makes it especially easy to structure your project in a way that promotes clean and efficient code. In this section, we'll dive into **best practices for code organization** and how to effectively manage dependencies using Go's built-in tool go get.

Best Practices for Code Organization in Go

The way you structure your Go projects greatly affects the ease with which you can scale, maintain, and collaborate on your codebase. Go provides a **minimalistic and simple project structure** by design, but it's essential to follow some conventions to ensure your code remains organized and clean as it grows.

Here are some best practices to consider when organizing your Go code:

1. Organize by Feature, Not Layer

While many languages encourage organizing code by technical layer (e.g., controllers, services, data access), Go encourages a **feature-based approach**. This means that instead of organizing your project by function (e.g., models, controllers, views), you should organize it based on features.

For example:

go
CopyEdit

```
/project
  /users
    handler.go
    service.go
    repository.go
  /orders
    handler.go
    service.go
    repository.go
  /auth
    handler.go
    service.go
```

Here:

- Each folder (/users, /orders, /auth) corresponds to a feature of the application, and inside it, you'll have files that define the specific logic for that feature. This keeps related code in one place and helps to prevent large, bloated folders.

2. Group Similar Code in Packages

Go's minimalistic approach to packages means that you can easily organize code into reusable packages. You should aim to create packages that logically encapsulate functionality.

For example, in a web service, you might create packages such as:

- /handlers: for request handlers and controllers.
- /models: for data structures that represent your domain entities.
- /services: for the business logic.
- /repositories: for database interaction logic.
- /utils: for utility functions, such as logging or string manipulation.

This helps to decouple components and promotes modularity in your project.

3. Use Meaningful Names for Packages and Functions

Go has a strong convention around naming. Here are some tips:

- **Package names should be short, descriptive, and lowercase**. For example, auth, user, order, etc. This helps ensure your code is clean and easy to navigate.
- **Function names** should be descriptive of what they do. Avoid one-word function names unless they are clear, such as Print() or Execute().
- **Method names** should follow the Go idiom of short and meaningful names. For example, CreateUser(), GetOrder().

4. Keep Your main Package Simple

The main package should be as simple as possible. Its purpose is to initiate and start the program, not to contain application logic. All the business logic should be abstracted into other packages.

For example:

go
CopyEdit
// main.go
package main

```
import (
    "fmt"
    "project/users"
    "project/orders"
)
func main() {
    user := users.NewUser("John Doe")
    order := orders.NewOrder(user, 100.50)

    fmt.Println(user)
    fmt.Println(order)
}
```

This keeps the entry point clean, allowing you to focus on the core functionality within the individual packages.

Managing Dependencies with go get

In Go, managing external dependencies is essential for keeping your project up to date with the libraries you rely on. Go Modules provide an efficient and simple way to manage these dependencies, and the go get command is one of the primary tools for fetching and managing them.

What is go get?

go get is a command that allows you to:

- Download and install Go packages (both standard library and third-party libraries).
- Update your dependencies to the latest version.

- Add packages to your project's module dependencies.

When you use go get, it automatically:

1. Downloads the package into your Go workspace.
2. Updates the go.mod and go.sum files to reflect the new dependency.
3. Installs the package so that it can be used by your project.

How to Use go get

To install a package, simply run:

bash
CopyEdit
go get github.com/gorilla/mux

This will:

- Download the gorilla/mux package.
- Add it to your go.mod file.
- Update your go.sum file to reflect the cryptographic hash of the downloaded package.

Adding a Specific Version

You can also specify a version of a dependency. For example, to install version v1.8.0 of the gorilla/mux package, use:

bash
CopyEdit
go get github.com/gorilla/mux@v1.8.0

This will update your go.mod file to use that specific version.

To update to the latest version of a package, use:

bash

CopyEdit

```
go get -u github.com/gorilla/mux
```

The -u flag will ensure that Go fetches the latest minor or patch version available.

Using Go Modules with go get

Go Modules make dependency management much simpler. In a Go project using modules, the go get command handles adding, removing, and updating dependencies within your go.mod file. If you haven't yet initialized Go Modules for your project, you can do so by running:

bash

CopyEdit

```
go mod init <module-name>
```

This creates the go.mod file at the root of your project, which keeps track of all the dependencies in your project.

After initializing your module, you can use go get to add any external dependencies you need.

Removing Unused Dependencies

If you have dependencies in your go.mod file that are no longer needed, Go provides a simple command to remove them:

bash

CopyEdit

```
go mod tidy
```

This command:

- Cleans up your go.mod file by removing any dependencies that are no longer required.
- Removes any extraneous dependencies in the go.sum file that are not being used by your project.

Viewing Dependencies

You can check the status of your dependencies at any time by running:

bash

CopyEdit

```
go list -m all
```

This will display a list of all the modules your project depends on, including their versions. This is useful for auditing the libraries your project relies on and for ensuring everything is up to date.

Go Proxy for Dependency Management

Go 1.11 introduced the Go Proxy feature, which caches dependencies to ensure they are fetched quickly and reliably. By default, Go will use proxy.golang.org to download modules, but you can configure it to use a different proxy if needed.

To disable the proxy and fetch directly from the source, use:

bash

CopyEdit

```
go env -w GOPROXY=direct
```

This ensures that Go fetches dependencies directly from their source repositories instead of relying on a proxy.

---

1. **Organize Your Code by Features**: Group related functionality together in packages to maintain a clean, modular structure. This will make your codebase more maintainable as it grows.

2. **Naming Conventions Matter**: Stick to Go idioms for naming packages, functions, and variables. Keep names short, descriptive, and consistent.

3. **Keep main Simple**: The main function should only initialize and run the application. The core logic should reside in separate packages.

4. **Manage Dependencies with go get**: Use go get to install, update, and manage your project's external dependencies.

5. **Use Go Modules**: Go Modules allow you to manage your project's dependencies efficiently, ensuring you are always using the right versions of external libraries.

6. **Clean Up Unused Dependencies**: Use go mod tidy to keep your dependencies up to date and remove any that are no longer needed.

Chapter 8: Concurrency in Go: Goroutines and Channels

Concurrency is one of the standout features of Go, enabling developers to write programs that can execute multiple tasks simultaneously. With the rise of multi-core processors and the need for high-performance, scalable applications, concurrency has become a critical feature in modern programming. Go's concurrency model is designed to be simple yet powerful, making it a compelling choice for building systems that need to handle multiple tasks at once.

In this chapter, we will explore Go's concurrency model, particularly **goroutines** and **channels**, and how they make concurrent programming straightforward and efficient. We'll also cover why concurrency is vital and how Go's approach simplifies the development of concurrent applications.

What is Concurrency? Why It Matters in Go

Before diving into Go's concurrency features, it's important to understand what concurrency is and why it matters in modern programming.

Understanding Concurrency

Concurrency refers to the ability of a program to handle multiple tasks at the same time. While many programs execute instructions sequentially (one task after another), a concurrent program is able to start working on one task, pause it, and then start working on another task before the first one finishes. This doesn't mean that the program executes these tasks at the exact same time (that would be parallelism), but rather that it can manage and switch between tasks efficiently.

193

In practice, concurrency is crucial for:

- **Responsive applications**: For example, a web server can handle multiple user requests simultaneously.
- **I/O-bound tasks**: Operations like reading from a file or making HTTP requests can be done concurrently without blocking the main application.
- **Better resource utilization**: With concurrency, applications can make better use of system resources, such as CPU cores, improving performance.

In Go, concurrency is a key feature, and it's baked into the language itself. Go provides **goroutines** and **channels**, two powerful abstractions that make concurrent programming easier than in many other languages.

Why Concurrency Matters in Go

Go was designed with concurrency in mind. Its lightweight goroutines and efficient channels help developers write high-performance, scalable applications that can handle thousands or even millions of concurrent tasks.

Go's approach to concurrency has several advantages:

- **Simplicity**: Go's concurrency model is simple to use and understand. With goroutines and channels, you can write concurrent code without getting bogged down in complex threading libraries or synchronization issues.
- **Performance**: Go's goroutines are extremely lightweight and can be spawned in large numbers with minimal memory overhead. This makes it possible to handle a high volume of concurrent tasks efficiently.
- **Ease of Use**: The concurrency model in Go is easy to implement. You don't need to worry about manual memory management, thread synchronization, or managing thread pools. Go's scheduler handles the heavy lifting.

In the next section, we'll explore **goroutines**, Go's lightweight thread mechanism that powers concurrent execution.

Understanding Goroutines: Lightweight Threads

A **goroutine** is the Go equivalent of a thread, but it's much more lightweight. Goroutines allow you to run functions concurrently without worrying about the overhead typically associated with threads in other programming languages.

What Makes Goroutines Lightweight?

Unlike threads in many other languages, which have a significant amount of overhead in terms of memory and operating system resources, goroutines are designed to be **extremely lightweight**. Here's how:

- **Stack Size**: A goroutine begins with a very small stack size (typically around 2 KB). As the goroutine executes, the stack grows and shrinks as needed, based on the function's requirements.
- **Multiplexing**: Go's runtime scheduler multiplexes many goroutines onto a smaller number of OS threads. It efficiently switches between goroutines, making it possible to execute thousands (or even millions) of them concurrently without putting a significant load on the system.

This lightweight nature of goroutines makes them incredibly efficient for handling tasks that would be costly in terms of resources when using traditional threads.

How to Create a Goroutine

Creating a goroutine is simple in Go. All you need to do is prepend the go keyword to any function call, and Go will run it concurrently.

For example:

go
CopyEdit

```go
package main

import (
    "fmt"
    "time"
)

func printNumbers() {
    for i := 1; i <= 5; i++ {
        fmt.Println(i)
        time.Sleep(time.Second)
    }
}

func main() {
    // Launch a goroutine
    go printNumbers()

    // Main goroutine continues to run concurrently
    fmt.Println("Main goroutine running")
    time.Sleep(6 * time.Second) // Wait for the goroutine to finish
}
```

In the code above:

- go printNumbers() launches the printNumbers function as a goroutine.
- The main function continues to run concurrently while the printNumbers function executes in the background.
- time.Sleep(6 * time.Second) is used to ensure the main function doesn't exit before the goroutine finishes.

When you run the program, you will see that the main goroutine prints "Main goroutine running" while the printNumbers goroutine is printing numbers. This is a simple example of concurrency in action.

Managing Goroutines

Since Go's goroutines are managed by the Go runtime, they don't require explicit synchronization mechanisms like locks or semaphores. The Go scheduler ensures that goroutines are executed efficiently and safely. However, when multiple goroutines need to communicate or share data, Go provides another critical tool: **channels**.

What are Channels?

Channels are the primary way in which goroutines communicate with each other in Go. A channel allows you to pass data between goroutines safely, and it is the key to writing concurrent Go programs that avoid common pitfalls like race conditions.

Creating and Using Channels

To use channels, you first need to create one. This is done using the make function:

go
CopyEdit

```go
ch := make(chan int)
```

Here, ch is a channel that will carry integer values. Once a channel is created, you can **send** and **receive** data through it.

- **Sending data** to a channel:

go
CopyEdit
```go
ch <- 42 // Send 42 to the channel
```

- **Receiving data** from a channel:

go
CopyEdit
```go
value := <-ch // Receive data from the channel
```

Here's an example where two goroutines communicate via a channel:

go
CopyEdit
```go
package main

import (
    "fmt"
    "time"
)

func sendData(ch chan int) {
```

```go
    fmt.Println("Sending data to the channel")
    ch <- 42
}

func main() {
    ch := make(chan int)

    // Launch goroutine
    go sendData(ch)

    // Receive data from channel
    value := <-ch
    fmt.Println("Received data:", value)

    time.Sleep(1 * time.Second) // Wait for goroutine to finish
}
```

In the example:

- A goroutine sends data (42) into the channel ch.
- The main goroutine receives that data and prints it.

Buffered Channels

By default, channels in Go are **unbuffered**, meaning that data can only be sent through them if another goroutine is ready to receive it. However, Go also supports **buffered channels**, which allow you to send data into the channel without blocking the sender (as long as the buffer is not full).

Creating a buffered channel is simple:

go
CopyEdit
```go
ch := make(chan int, 2) // Channel with a buffer size of 2
```

In this case, you can send up to two values into the channel without blocking. If the buffer is full, any further sends will block until space becomes available.

Channels as Synchronization Tools

In addition to allowing goroutines to communicate, channels also act as a synchronization mechanism. If a goroutine is waiting to receive data from a channel, it is **blocked** until data is available. This can be used to synchronize goroutines effectively.

For example:

go
CopyEdit
```go
package main

import (
    "fmt"
)

func task(ch chan bool) {
    fmt.Println("Performing task...")
    ch <- true // Signal that the task is complete
}
```

```go
func main() {
    ch := make(chan bool)

    // Launch goroutine
    go task(ch)

    // Wait for the task to complete
    <-ch
    fmt.Println("Task completed!")
}
```

In this code:

- The main goroutine launches the task function as a goroutine.
- The task goroutine sends a true value to the channel when it finishes.
- The main goroutine waits for the signal before printing "Task completed!"

- **Concurrency in Go** is achieved using **goroutines**, which are lightweight threads managed by the Go runtime. They allow your application to perform multiple tasks simultaneously without the overhead of traditional threads.
- **Channels** are used to communicate between goroutines, enabling safe data sharing without the need for complex synchronization mechanisms.
- Go's concurrency model is **simple, efficient, and safe**, making it an excellent choice for writing highly scalable, performant applications.

Working with Channels for Safe Data Sharing

Channels in Go are the primary way for goroutines to communicate with one another. They provide a **safe, synchronized** way to share data between concurrent goroutines, and their design ensures that data exchange is **free from race conditions**.

A **race condition** occurs when two or more goroutines access shared data at the same time, and at least one of them is modifying the data. This can lead to unexpected behavior, bugs, or crashes. However, Go's channels help solve this issue by ensuring that only one goroutine can send data to the channel at a time and only one goroutine can receive data from it at a time.

Why Use Channels for Data Sharing?

1. **Safety**: Since channels provide a built-in mechanism for synchronization, they eliminate the need for other synchronization tools, like locks or mutexes. You don't need to worry about manually protecting shared data when using channels.
2. **Synchronization**: Channels implicitly synchronize the sending and receiving of data. This means that a goroutine will block when sending data to a channel if there is no other goroutine ready to receive the data, and vice versa. This provides a **natural synchronization** mechanism without requiring manual intervention.
3. **Communication**: Channels allow goroutines to communicate directly. By passing values through a channel, you can build complex systems that involve multiple goroutines working together, passing data back and forth as they complete different tasks.

Let's consider an example where multiple goroutines share data via a channel.

go

```go
package main

import (
    "fmt"
    "time"
)

func worker(id int, ch chan string) {
    // Simulate some work
    fmt.Printf("Worker %d started\n", id)
    time.Sleep(2 * time.Second)

    // Send a message back to the channel
    ch <- fmt.Sprintf("Worker %d completed", id)
}

func main() {
    ch := make(chan string)
```

```go
// Start multiple goroutines

for i := 1; i <= 3; i++ {

    go worker(i, ch)

}


// Receive messages from the channel

for i := 1; i <= 3; i++ {

    msg := <-ch

    fmt.Println(msg)

}

}
```

In this example:

- The worker function simulates work by sleeping for 2 seconds and then sending a message back to the channel.
- The main goroutine waits for messages from the channel, ensuring that it processes the completion messages from each worker sequentially.
- The program guarantees that the goroutines communicate and synchronize safely without any race conditions.

Buffered vs. Unbuffered Channels

Channels can either be **unbuffered** or **buffered**, and the choice between the two has significant implications for how data is passed and how goroutines are synchronized. Let's explore the differences.

Unbuffered Channels

An **unbuffered channel** is the simplest type of channel in Go. When you send data to an unbuffered channel, the sender goroutine will block until there is a receiver ready to accept the data. Similarly, if you try to receive from an unbuffered channel but no data is available, the receiver will block until a sender sends data.

Unbuffered channels are ideal when you want to **synchronize** the sender and receiver explicitly. They are often used for **synchronization primitives**, where you want one goroutine to wait for another before proceeding.

Example of Unbuffered Channel:

go

CopyEdit

```
package main


import (

    "fmt"
```

```go
    "time"

)


func producer(ch chan int) {

    fmt.Println("Producer started")

    time.Sleep(1 * time.Second) // Simulate work

    ch <- 42                // Send data to channel

    fmt.Println("Producer finished")

}


func consumer(ch chan int) {

    fmt.Println("Consumer started")

    data := <-ch            // Receive data from channel

    fmt.Printf("Consumer received: %d\n", data)

    fmt.Println("Consumer finished")

}


func main() {

    ch := make(chan int) // Unbuffered channel
```

```
// Start goroutines

go producer(ch)

go consumer(ch)


// Wait for goroutines to complete

time.Sleep(2 * time.Second)

}
```

In the example above:

- The producer goroutine sends an integer (42) to the channel, but it won't proceed until the consumer goroutine is ready to receive the data.
- The consumer goroutine blocks until data is available in the channel.
- This synchronization ensures that the consumer always receives data after the producer has finished.

Buffered Channels

A **buffered channel** allows you to send data without blocking, as long as there is space in the buffer. You can think of a buffered channel as a queue. When data is sent to the channel, it is placed into the buffer, and the sender can continue executing without being blocked (unless the buffer is full). Similarly, when data is received from the channel, it is removed from the buffer.

Buffered channels are useful when you want to decouple the sender and receiver to some extent, allowing them to operate independently without blocking immediately.

You can create a buffered channel by specifying the **buffer size** when calling make.

go

CopyEdit

```
ch := make(chan int, 2) // Buffered channel with a capacity of 2
```

Example of Buffered Channel:

go

CopyEdit

```
package main

import (
    "fmt"
)

func producer(ch chan int) {
    fmt.Println("Producer started")
    ch <- 42
```

```go
    fmt.Println("Producer sent data")

    ch <- 43

    fmt.Println("Producer sent data again")

}


func consumer(ch chan int) {

    fmt.Println("Consumer started")

    data1 := <-ch

    fmt.Printf("Consumer received: %d\n", data1)

    data2 := <-ch

    fmt.Printf("Consumer received: %d\n", data2)

    fmt.Println("Consumer finished")

}


func main() {

    ch := make(chan int, 2) // Create a buffered channel


    // Start goroutines

    go producer(ch)
```

```go
go consumer(ch)


// Wait for goroutines to finish

fmt.Scanln()

}
```

In this example:

- The producer sends two values into the buffered channel without blocking because the buffer has a capacity of 2.
- The consumer then receives both values from the channel.
- The program doesn't block between the sender and receiver since the buffered channel allows a small buffer for the sender to store data.

When to Use Buffered vs. Unbuffered Channels

The decision to use an unbuffered or buffered channel depends on the needs of your application:

- **Unbuffered channels** are best when you want to **synchronize** the sender and receiver. The sender will block until the receiver is ready, ensuring that the sender does not send more data than the receiver can process at a time.
- **Buffered channels** are useful when you want to allow some **decoupling** between the sender and receiver. The sender can continue producing data and the receiver can consume it at a later time. Buffered channels are also great for reducing the risk of **deadlocks**, as they allow more flexibility in how data is transferred.

In general, unbuffered channels are more straightforward for tightly coupled tasks, while buffered channels are better suited for tasks that can tolerate some delay or have varying rates of production and consumption.

- **Channels** are a critical component in Go for safe, synchronized communication between goroutines. They eliminate the need for complex synchronization mechanisms like mutexes and locks.
- **Unbuffered channels** ensure strict synchronization between the sender and receiver, blocking until the other party is ready.
- **Buffered channels** allow for more flexibility by enabling the sender to continue sending data as long as there is space in the buffer. They are ideal for decoupling producers and consumers.
- By using channels correctly, you can build highly concurrent programs in Go that are both **efficient** and **safe**, without the usual pitfalls associated with shared memory access in multi-threaded applications.

Synchronizing Goroutines with sync.WaitGroup

In concurrent programming, especially when you're working with multiple goroutines, there's often a need to wait for all the goroutines to finish before moving on to the next step in your program. The sync.WaitGroup in Go provides a simple and effective way to handle this.

A WaitGroup allows you to wait for a collection of goroutines to finish executing. It maintains a counter that tracks how many goroutines are still running. Each time a goroutine is launched, you **add** to the WaitGroup, and when the goroutine finishes, you **decrement** the counter. Once the counter reaches zero, the program proceeds to the next step.

How to Use sync.WaitGroup

1. **Create a WaitGroup**: You start by declaring a WaitGroup variable.
2. **Add to the WaitGroup**: Every time a new goroutine is launched, you increment the counter using wg.Add(1).
3. **Decrement when goroutine finishes**: Inside each goroutine, call defer wg.Done() to decrement the counter once the goroutine is done.
4. **Wait for all goroutines to finish**: Finally, you use wg.Wait() to block the main program until the counter reaches zero (i.e., all goroutines are finished).

Example of Using sync.WaitGroup:

go

CopyEdit

```
package main

import (

    "fmt"

    "sync"

    "time"

)


func worker(id int, wg *sync.WaitGroup) {

    defer wg.Done() // Decrement the counter when the goroutine finishes
```

```go
        // Simulate work
        fmt.Printf("Worker %d started\n", id)
        time.Sleep(time.Second)
        fmt.Printf("Worker %d finished\n", id)
}


func main() {
        var wg sync.WaitGroup


        // Start multiple goroutines
        for i := 1; i <= 3; i++ {
                wg.Add(1) // Increment the counter for each new goroutine
                go worker(i, &wg)
        }


        // Wait for all goroutines to finish
        wg.Wait()
        fmt.Println("All workers finished!")
```

Explanation:

- We create a WaitGroup called wg.
- Each time we start a new goroutine, we call wg.Add(1) to increment the counter.
- Inside each goroutine, we call defer wg.Done() to ensure that the counter is decremented once the goroutine completes.
- The wg.Wait() in the main function blocks until the counter reaches zero, ensuring that the program doesn't exit before all goroutines finish.

Common Use Case: Waiting for Multiple Goroutines to Finish

The sync.WaitGroup is most often used in scenarios where you want to launch multiple goroutines to perform concurrent tasks (e.g., making multiple API calls, processing data in parallel) and then wait for all of them to complete before proceeding with the next step.

The select Statement for Managing Multiple Channels

When working with concurrency in Go, you'll often have to deal with multiple channels simultaneously. The select **statement** is a powerful tool in Go for handling multiple channels concurrently. It allows you to wait on multiple channels and process data from whichever channel is ready.

How the select Statement Works

The select statement works similarly to a switch statement, but instead of evaluating cases with constant values, it evaluates channels. It waits for one of the channels to be ready for sending or receiving data. When one of the channels becomes ready, the corresponding case block is executed.

1. **Blocking on Multiple Channels**: If none of the channels are ready, the select statement will block, waiting for one of the channels to become available.
2. **Random Selection**: If multiple channels are ready, select will randomly pick one to execute. This helps prevent any single channel from being favored over others.

Basic Syntax of select

go

CopyEdit

```
select {

case msg1 := <-ch1:

    fmt.Println("Received", msg1)

case msg2 := <-ch2:

    fmt.Println("Received", msg2)

case <-time.After(time.Second):

    fmt.Println("Timeout")

}
```

- If ch1 becomes ready to send data, the first case will execute.
- If ch2 becomes ready, the second case will execute.
- If neither channel is ready within 1 second, the time.After case will be triggered.

Example: Using select with Multiple Channels

Let's look at an example where we use select to listen to multiple channels concurrently:

go

CopyEdit

```
package main

import (
    "fmt"
    "time"
)

func sendData(ch chan string, delay time.Duration) {
    time.Sleep(delay)
    ch <- "Data received"
}
```

```go
func main() {

    ch1 := make(chan string)

    ch2 := make(chan string)


    go sendData(ch1, 3*time.Second)

    go sendData(ch2, 1*time.Second)


    // Using select to handle multiple channels

    select {

    case msg1 := <-ch1:

        fmt.Println("From ch1:", msg1)

    case msg2 := <-ch2:

        fmt.Println("From ch2:", msg2)

    case <-time.After(2 * time.Second):

        fmt.Println("Timeout: No message received in time")

    }

}
```

Explanation:

- We define two channels, ch1 and ch2.
- The sendData function simulates work by sleeping for a specified duration before sending data into the channel.
- The select statement listens to both channels.
- ch1 has a delay of 3 seconds, and ch2 has a delay of 1 second.
- Since ch2 is ready first, the message from ch2 is printed. If no message is received within 2 seconds, the timeout case is triggered.

Use Cases for select

1. **Timeouts and Cancellation**: select is useful for implementing timeouts and cancellation logic in concurrent applications. You can use the time.After function or a cancellation signal channel to handle timeouts in a non-blocking way.

2. **Handling Multiple Input Channels**: If you're waiting for input from multiple sources, such as multiple users, multiple sensors, or multiple external systems, the select statement allows you to efficiently manage all those inputs concurrently.

3. **Broadcasting and Fan-Out**: The select statement can be used in producer-consumer models where data is sent to multiple goroutines, and you want to handle the data as it arrives, from whichever goroutine finishes first.

- **sync.WaitGroup** is a convenient way to synchronize the completion of multiple goroutines. It ensures that your program waits for all goroutines to finish their work before proceeding to the next step.
- **select** is an invaluable tool for managing multiple channels concurrently. It lets you listen to several channels at once and handle whichever one becomes ready

first. It also supports timeouts and cancellation, making it essential for managing concurrent tasks that involve multiple sources of input.

- **Use sync.WaitGroup** when you need to wait for multiple goroutines to finish their work before proceeding. It's ideal for scenarios where you have multiple tasks running in parallel, and you need to wait for all of them to complete before moving forward.
- **Use select** when dealing with multiple channels and you need to take action based on whichever channel provides data first. It's perfect for handling concurrent operations that involve different sources of input.

Common Concurrency Patterns in Go

When building concurrent applications in Go, there are several common patterns that help manage and coordinate multiple goroutines efficiently. These patterns are foundational to writing scalable and maintainable concurrent code. Let's explore some of the most popular concurrency patterns in Go and how they can be applied in different scenarios.

1. Worker Pool Pattern

The **worker pool pattern** is used when you have a collection of tasks that need to be executed concurrently, but you want to limit the number of concurrently running workers to avoid overwhelming the system. This pattern is useful in scenarios where tasks are CPU-bound, I/O-bound, or network-bound, and you want to ensure that your system can handle a large number of tasks without running out of resources.

In this pattern, a fixed number of workers (goroutines) are created. Each worker listens on a shared channel for tasks. When a task becomes available, the worker picks it up and executes it. If a task finishes, the worker checks back for more work.

Example: Worker Pool

go

CopyEdit

```go
package main

import (
    "fmt"
    "time"
)

func worker(id int, jobs <-chan int, results chan<- int) {
    for job := range jobs {
        fmt.Printf("Worker %d started job %d\n", id, job)
        time.Sleep(time.Second) // Simulate work
        results <- job * 2
        fmt.Printf("Worker %d finished job %d\n", id, job)
    }
}
```

```go
func main() {

    const numWorkers = 3

    jobs := make(chan int, 5)

    results := make(chan int, 5)


    // Start workers
    for i := 1; i <= numWorkers; i++ {

        go worker(i, jobs, results)

    }
    // Send tasks to the workers
    for j := 1; j <= 5; j++ {

        jobs <- j

    }
    close(jobs)
    // Collect results
    for a := 1; a <= 5; a++ {

        fmt.Println("Result:", <-results)

    }

}
```

Explanation:

- We create a fixed number of workers (3 workers in this case).
- The jobs channel is used to send tasks to the workers, and the results channel collects the results.
- Each worker listens for tasks from the jobs channel, performs the task, and then sends the result to the results channel.
- The main function sends tasks to the workers and waits for the results.

This pattern allows you to efficiently manage a pool of workers that can process a large number of tasks without overloading the system.

2. Fan-out, Fan-in Pattern

The **fan-out, fan-in** pattern is useful when you need to distribute tasks to multiple workers (fan-out), and then collect the results from all the workers (fan-in). This pattern can be used to parallelize data processing or computations.

- **Fan-out**: Distribute tasks to multiple goroutines.
- **Fan-in**: Collect the results from all the goroutines.

Example: Fan-out, Fan-in

go

CopyEdit

```
package main

import (

    "fmt"

    "time"
```

```go
)

func processData(data int, result chan<- int) {

    time.Sleep(time.Second) // Simulate work

    result <- data * 2

}

func main() {

    data := []int{1, 2, 3, 4, 5}

    result := make(chan int, len(data))

    // Fan-out: Distribute work to multiple goroutines

    for _, d := range data {

        go processData(d, result)

    }

    // Fan-in: Collect results

    for i := 0; i < len(data); i++ {

        fmt.Println("Processed Result:", <-result)

    }

}
```

Explanation:

- The processData function simulates processing each data item (multiplying it by 2).
- We distribute the work (fan-out) by spawning a goroutine for each item in the data slice.
- We then collect the results (fan-in) by reading from the result channel.
- This pattern is ideal for cases where you have multiple independent tasks that can be processed concurrently, and you need to gather the results afterward.

3. Publish-Subscribe Pattern

The **publish-subscribe (pub/sub) pattern** is used when you need to broadcast messages from one source (the publisher) to multiple subscribers. In Go, this pattern is usually implemented using channels, where the publisher sends data to a channel, and multiple subscribers receive that data.

Example: Publish-Subscribe

go

CopyEdit

```
package main

import (

    "fmt"

    "time"

)
```

```go
func publisher(ch chan<- string) {

    messages := []string{"Hello", "World", "Go", "Is", "Great"}

    for _, msg := range messages {

        ch <- msg

        time.Sleep(500 * time.Millisecond) // Simulate a delay

    }

    close(ch)

}


func subscriber(id int, ch <-chan string) {

    for msg := range ch {

        fmt.Printf("Subscriber %d received: %s\n", id, msg)

    }

}


func main() {

    ch := make(chan string)
```

```
// Start the publisher and two subscribers

go publisher(ch)

go subscriber(1, ch)

go subscriber(2, ch)

// Allow time for subscribers to receive messages

time.Sleep(3 * time.Second)

}
```

Explanation:

- The publisher function sends a series of messages to the channel.
- The subscriber function listens on the channel and prints any messages it receives.
- Multiple subscribers can receive the same message broadcasted by the publisher.

This pattern is commonly used in event-driven systems where multiple components need to react to the same event.

Pitfalls and Debugging Concurrency Issues

While Go's concurrency model is powerful, working with goroutines and channels can introduce various pitfalls. Let's discuss some common concurrency issues and how to debug them effectively.

1. Race Conditions

A **race condition** occurs when two or more goroutines access shared data concurrently, and at least one of them modifies the data. This can lead to unpredictable behavior and bugs that are difficult to reproduce.

Example of a Race Condition:

go

CopyEdit

```
package main

import (
    "fmt"
    "sync"
)

func main() {
    var counter int
    var wg sync.WaitGroup

    for i := 0; i < 1000; i++ {
```

```go
    wg.Add(1)

    go func() {

        counter++

        wg.Done()

    }()

    }

    wg.Wait()

    fmt.Println("Counter:", counter)

}
```

Explanation:

- In this code, 1,000 goroutines concurrently increment the counter variable. Since multiple goroutines are modifying the counter at the same time, the result can be unpredictable, and the final output may not be 1,000.

Solution:

- Use synchronization mechanisms like **mutexes** or **channels** to ensure that only one goroutine modifies the data at a time.

Fixed Example Using Mutex:

go

CopyEdit

```go
package main
```

```go
import (

    "fmt"

    "sync"

)


func main() {

    var counter int

    var wg sync.WaitGroup

    var mu sync.Mutex


    for i := 0; i < 1000; i++ {

        wg.Add(1)

        go func() {

            mu.Lock()

            counter++

            mu.Unlock()

            wg.Done()

        }()
```

```
    }

    wg.Wait()

    fmt.Println("Counter:", counter)

}
```

2. Deadlocks

A **deadlock** occurs when two or more goroutines are blocked forever because they are each waiting on each other to release a resource. This can happen when channels are used improperly or when a goroutine waits for a resource that will never be released.

Example of a Deadlock:

go

CopyEdit

```
package main

import "fmt"

func main() {
    ch1 := make(chan string)
```

```go
ch2 := make(chan string)

go func() {

    ch1 <- "Hello"

    ch2 <- "World"

}()


fmt.Println(<-ch1) // This will block

fmt.Println(<-ch2) // This will also block

}
```

Explanation:

- The main function is waiting on two channels (ch1 and ch2), but the goroutine will never send data to these channels because it's waiting on them to be read.

Solution:

- Ensure that channels are properly handled with appropriate goroutines to avoid waiting on each other indefinitely.

3. Debugging Concurrency

Debugging concurrency issues can be challenging due to the non-deterministic nature of goroutines. However, there are tools and strategies to help:

231

Use the -race flag: The -race flag detects race conditions during execution.

bash

CopyEdit

```
go run -race main.go
```

1.

2. **Log Goroutine States**: Adding logging can help track the state of each goroutine and understand where things are going wrong.

Go Trace: Use Go's built-in tracing tool to track goroutine activity and performance.

bash

CopyEdit

```
go tool trace trace.out
```

3.

4. **Goroutine Dumps**: In case of deadlocks or unexpected behavior, a goroutine dump can help you understand the state of all goroutines at a given point.

- **Worker Pool**: Limit concurrent workers to optimize system resources.
- **Fan-out, Fan-in**: Distribute work to multiple goroutines and collect the results.
- **Publish-Subscribe**: Broadcast messages to multiple listeners.
- **Pitfalls**: Watch out for race conditions and deadlocks.
- **Debugging**: Use the -race flag, logging, and Go's tracing tools to debug concurrency issues.

Go provides powerful concurrency primitives that allow you to write efficient and scalable applications. However, concurrency comes with its own set of challenges, and understanding these patterns and potential pitfalls will help you write more reliable and performant Go code.

Chapter 9: File Handling and Working with JSON

In this chapter, we'll explore how to work with files and directories in Go, as well as how to read, write, and manipulate JSON data. These are fundamental tasks when developing real-world applications, as data is often stored in files or exchanged using JSON.

Reading and Writing Files in Go

Go provides a simple and efficient way to handle files with the os and io/ioutil packages. You can read from and write to files using built-in functions.

1. Reading Files

To read a file, we typically use the os.Open function to open the file and then Read or ReadFile to read its contents.

Example: Reading a File

go
CopyEdit
```
package main

import (
    "fmt"
    "io/ioutil"
    "log"
)
```

```go
func main() {
    data, err := ioutil.ReadFile("example.txt")
    if err != nil {
        log.Fatal(err)
    }
    fmt.Println("File Contents:")
    fmt.Println(string(data))
}
```

Explanation:

- The ioutil.ReadFile function reads the entire content of the file example.txt into a byte slice.
- The string(data) converts the byte slice into a string, which is then printed.
- If there's an error, the program logs the error and exits.

2. Writing Files

To write data to a file, we can use os.Create to create a new file (or truncate an existing one) and Write or WriteString to write the contents.

Example: Writing to a File

go
CopyEdit

```go
package main

import (
    "fmt"
    "os"
```

```go
)

func main() {
    file, err := os.Create("output.txt")
    if err != nil {
        fmt.Println("Error creating file:", err)
        return
    }
    defer file.Close() // Ensure the file is closed after writing

    content := "Hello, Go! Writing to a file is easy."
    _, err = file.WriteString(content)
    if err != nil {
        fmt.Println("Error writing to file:", err)
        return
    }

    fmt.Println("File written successfully")
}
```

Explanation:

- os.Create is used to create or truncate an existing file. It returns a file pointer, which we can use to write to the file.
- WriteString writes a string to the file.
- defer file.Close() ensures that the file is closed when the function returns, regardless of whether the operation is successful or not.

3. Appending to a File

To append data to an existing file, use os.OpenFile with the os.O_APPEND flag.

Example: Appending to a File

go
CopyEdit

```go
package main

import (
    "fmt"
    "os"
)

func main() {
    file, err := os.OpenFile("output.txt", os.O_APPEND|os.O_WRONLY, 0644)
    if err != nil {
        fmt.Println("Error opening file:", err)
        return
    }
    defer file.Close()

    content := "\nAppended content."
    _, err = file.WriteString(content)
    if err != nil {
        fmt.Println("Error appending to file:", err)
        return
    }
```

```go
    fmt.Println("Content appended successfully")
}
```

Explanation:

- os.OpenFile opens the file in append mode (os.O_APPEND) and write-only mode (os.O_WRONLY).
- The content is appended to the file, rather than overwriting it.

Working with Directories and File Paths

In Go, you can also work with directories, check for their existence, and manipulate file paths using the os and path/filepath packages.

1. Creating Directories

To create directories, you can use the os.Mkdir or os.MkdirAll function.

Example: Creating a Directory

go
CopyEdit

```go
package main

import (
    "fmt"
    "os"
)

func main() {
```

```go
err := os.Mkdir("new_directory", 0755)
if err != nil {
    fmt.Println("Error creating directory:", err)
    return
}
fmt.Println("Directory created successfully")
}
```

Explanation:

- os.Mkdir creates a single directory. The second argument (0755) sets the permissions for the directory (read, write, execute for the owner, and read/execute for others).
- If the directory already exists, an error will be returned.

2. Creating Nested Directories

If you want to create multiple levels of directories at once, use os.MkdirAll.

Example: Creating Nested Directories

go
CopyEdit
```go
package main

import (
    "fmt"
    "os"
)

func main() {
```

```go
err := os.MkdirAll("parent/child/grandchild", 0755)
if err != nil {
    fmt.Println("Error creating directories:", err)
    return
}
fmt.Println("Nested directories created successfully")
}
```

Explanation:

- os.MkdirAll creates all directories in the specified path. If any of the directories in the path already exist, it doesn't return an error.

3. Listing Files in a Directory

To list files in a directory, use os.ReadDir (introduced in Go 1.16) or ioutil.ReadDir (for older versions).

Example: Listing Files in a Directory

go
CopyEdit
```go
package main

import (
    "fmt"
    "os"
)

func main() {
    files, err := os.ReadDir(".")
```

```go
    if err != nil {
        fmt.Println("Error reading directory:", err)
        return
    }

    fmt.Println("Files in the current directory:")
    for _, file := range files {
        fmt.Println(file.Name())
    }
}
```

Explanation:

- os.ReadDir returns a list of directory entries (files and directories) in the specified directory ("." represents the current directory).
- The program iterates over the entries and prints their names.

4. Checking if a File Exists

Before performing operations on a file, it's common to check if the file exists.

Example: Checking File Existence

go
CopyEdit
```go
package main

import (
    "fmt"
    "os"
)
```

```go
func main() {
    _, err := os.Stat("example.txt")
    if os.IsNotExist(err) {
        fmt.Println("File does not exist")
    } else if err != nil {
        fmt.Println("Error checking file:", err)
    } else {
        fmt.Println("File exists")
    }
}
```

Explanation:

- os.Stat checks the file's status. If the file does not exist, os.IsNotExist(err) will return true.
- This is useful for conditionally performing actions based on file existence.

Working with JSON in Go

JSON (JavaScript Object Notation) is one of the most common formats for exchanging data between systems. Go provides built-in support for working with JSON through the encoding/json package.

1. Encoding Go Structs to JSON

You can convert Go structs to JSON using the json.Marshal function. This process is called **encoding**.

Example: Encoding Structs to JSON

go
CopyEdit

```go
package main

import (
    "encoding/json"
    "fmt"
)

type Person struct {
    Name string `json:"name"`
    Age  int    `json:"age"`
}

func main() {
    person := Person{Name: "John", Age: 30}

    jsonData, err := json.Marshal(person)
    if err != nil {
        fmt.Println("Error encoding JSON:", err)
        return
    }

    fmt.Println("JSON Data:", string(jsonData))
}
```

Explanation:

- The json.Marshal function converts the Person struct into a JSON-encoded byte slice.
- The struct tags (e.g., json:"name") specify the field names in the JSON data.

2. Decoding JSON into Go Structs

You can convert JSON data back into Go structs using the json.Unmarshal function. This process is called **decoding**.

Example: Decoding JSON to Structs

go
CopyEdit

```go
package main

import (
    "encoding/json"
    "fmt"
)

type Person struct {
    Name string `json:"name"`
    Age  int    `json:"age"`
}

func main() {
    jsonData := `{"name":"John", "age":30}`

    var person Person
```

243

```go
    err := json.Unmarshal([]byte(jsonData), &person)
    if err != nil {
        fmt.Println("Error decoding JSON:", err)
        return
    }

    fmt.Printf("Decoded Person: %+v\n", person)
}
```

Explanation:

- json.Unmarshal takes JSON data and decodes it into the person struct.
- The &person argument is a pointer to the struct where the decoded data will be stored.

3. Pretty-Printing JSON

For debugging or displaying JSON in a human-readable format, you can use json.MarshalIndent to pretty-print JSON data with indentation.

Example: Pretty-Printing JSON

go
CopyEdit
```go
package main

import (
    "encoding/json"
    "fmt"
)
```

```go
type Person struct {
    Name string `json:"name"`
    Age  int    `json:"age"`
}

func main() {
    person := Person{Name: "John", Age: 30}

    jsonData, err := json.MarshalIndent(person, "", "  ")
    if err != nil {
        fmt.Println("Error encoding JSON:", err)
        return
    }

    fmt.Println("Pretty JSON:")
    fmt.Println(string(jsonData))
}
```

Explanation:

- json.MarshalIndent formats the JSON output with indentation (" " for two spaces).
- This makes the JSON data easier to read and debug.

Working with files and JSON data is a key part of many Go programs. Go's simplicity and efficiency in handling these tasks make it an ideal choice for file manipulation and data processing. In this chapter, you learned how to read and write files, create and manage directories, and work with JSON using Go's built-in packages.

In this section, we'll dive deeper into encoding and decoding JSON data using Go's encoding/json package. Additionally, we'll explore how to handle CSV files, which are often used for data storage, import, and export in many applications.

Encoding and Decoding JSON

In Go, handling JSON data is straightforward with the encoding/json package. We already covered basic encoding and decoding in the previous section, but here we will delve deeper into how to work with more complex JSON data, including nested structures and arrays.

1. Encoding (Marshalling) Complex Data

To encode complex data, such as nested structs or arrays, you can follow the same principles as encoding simple structs. However, when dealing with nested data, Go will recursively encode the inner structs or arrays into JSON.

Example: Encoding Nested Structs to JSON

go

CopyEdit

```
package main

import (
```

```go
    "encoding/json"

    "fmt"

)


type Address struct {

    Street string `json:"street"`

    City   string `json:"city"`

}


type Person struct {

    Name    string `json:"name"`

    Age     int    `json:"age"`

    Address Address `json:"address"`

}


func main() {

    person := Person{

        Name: "Alice",

        Age:  28,
```

```go
        Address: Address{
            Street: "123 Main St",
            City:   "Wonderland",
        },
    }

    jsonData, err := json.Marshal(person)
    if err != nil {
        fmt.Println("Error encoding JSON:", err)
        return
    }

    fmt.Println("Encoded JSON:", string(jsonData))
}
```

Explanation:

- The Person struct contains an Address struct, which will be encoded as part of the JSON object.
- json.Marshal handles the nested structure and outputs a JSON string with nested fields.

Output:

json

CopyEdit

{"name":"Alice","age":28,"address":{"street":"123 Main St","city":"Wonderland"}}

2. Decoding (Unmarshalling) Complex Data

Similarly, decoding JSON into nested structs requires the use of pointers to the structs where the data will be stored. The json.Unmarshal function will recursively decode the JSON data and populate the fields of the corresponding structs.

Example: Decoding Nested JSON to Structs

go

CopyEdit

```go
package main

import (

    "encoding/json"

    "fmt"

)
```

```go
type Address struct {

    Street string `json:"street"`

    City   string `json:"city"`

}


type Person struct {

    Name    string `json:"name"`

    Age     int    `json:"age"`

    Address Address `json:"address"`

}


func main() {

    jsonData := `{"name":"Alice","age":28,"address":{"street":"123 Main St","city":"Wonderland"}}`


    var person Person

    err := json.Unmarshal([]byte(jsonData), &person)

    if err != nil {

        fmt.Println("Error decoding JSON:", err)
```

```
    return

}
```

```
fmt.Printf("Decoded Struct: %+v\n", person)

}
```

Explanation:

- The JSON string contains a nested object for the address field.
- The json.Unmarshal function takes the JSON data and decodes it into the Person struct, populating both the Address field and the basic fields (Name, Age).

Output:

css

CopyEdit

Decoded Struct: {Name:Alice Age:28 Address:{Street:123 Main St City:Wonderland}}

Parsing and Writing CSV Files

CSV (Comma-Separated Values) is a simple and widely-used format for data exchange, especially in spreadsheets or simple databases. Go provides built-in support for parsing and writing CSV data using the encoding/csv package.

1. Reading CSV Files

Reading a CSV file in Go is done through the csv.NewReader type, which can read records from a CSV file and return them as slices of strings. Each record corresponds to a line in the CSV file, and each field in the record corresponds to a cell in that line.

Example: Reading a CSV File

go

CopyEdit

```go
package main

import (
    "encoding/csv"
    "fmt"
    "os"
    "log"
)

func main() {
    file, err := os.Open("data.csv")
    if err != nil {
```

```go
        log.Fatal(err)

    }

    defer file.Close()


    reader := csv.NewReader(file)

    records, err := reader.ReadAll()

    if err != nil {

        log.Fatal(err)

    }


    for _, record := range records {

        fmt.Println(record)

    }

}
```

Explanation:

- os.Open opens the CSV file, and csv.NewReader(file) prepares the file for reading.
- ReadAll reads all the records at once into a slice of string slices (each slice corresponds to a record).

- Each record (which is a slice of strings) is printed to the console.

Sample data.csv content:

CopyEdit

Name,Age,City

Alice,28,Wonderland

Bob,35,Builderland

Output:

csharp

CopyEdit

[Name Age City]

[Alice 28 Wonderland]

[Bob 35 Builderland]

2. Writing to CSV Files

Writing to CSV files involves creating a csv.Writer object and using the Write or WriteAll method to write records (slices of strings) to a file.

Example: Writing to a CSV File

go

CopyEdit

```go
package main

import (

    "encoding/csv"

    "fmt"

    "os"

)


func main() {

    file, err := os.Create("output.csv")

    if err != nil {

        fmt.Println("Error creating file:", err)

        return

    }

    defer file.Close()


    writer := csv.NewWriter(file)

    defer writer.Flush() // Ensure all data is written to the file
```

```go
records := [][]string{

    {"Name", "Age", "City"},

    {"Alice", "28", "Wonderland"},

    {"Bob", "35", "Builderland"},

}

for _, record := range records {

    err := writer.Write(record)

    if err != nil {

        fmt.Println("Error writing record:", err)

    }

}

fmt.Println("CSV file written successfully")

}
```

Explanation:

- os.Create creates a new CSV file.
- csv.NewWriter(file) initializes the CSV writer.
- Each record is written with writer.Write(). The Write method takes a slice of strings and writes them as a CSV row.

- The `defer writer.Flush()` ensures that all the buffered data is written to the file when the function completes.

Output:

- A file named `output.csv` will be created with the following content:

CopyEdit

Name,Age,City

Alice,28,Wonderland

Bob,35,Builderland

In this section, we explored how to encode and decode JSON data in Go, focusing on handling complex, nested structures. We also learned how to read from and write to CSV files, another essential format for data handling in many applications.

Handling files and JSON data efficiently is key to creating robust applications, and Go provides simple yet powerful tools for these tasks. In the next section, we will continue exploring more advanced file handling techniques, including handling large files and managing error handling during file operations.

Chapter 10: Building a Command-Line (CLI) Tool in Go

Command-line tools are one of the most common and powerful ways to interact with a computer system, offering a lightweight and efficient interface for users and developers alike. In this chapter, we will explore how to build a simple yet powerful Command-Line Interface (CLI) tool using Go.

Why Go is Great for CLI Applications

Go is an excellent choice for building CLI applications for several reasons:

1. **Simplicity and Readability**: Go's syntax is clean and easy to understand. With minimalistic designs, Go allows developers to focus on solving problems without dealing with unnecessary complexity.

2. **Fast Execution**: Go is a compiled language, and its programs run quickly. For CLI tools, performance is key—whether you are processing files, making API calls, or running scripts—Go ensures your application is responsive.

3. **Concurrency**: With its built-in concurrency model (goroutines and channels), Go makes it easy to handle multiple tasks in parallel, which is a frequent requirement for CLI tools that need to handle several operations simultaneously.

4. **Cross-Platform Compatibility**: Go supports cross-compilation, allowing you to compile your program for various platforms (Windows, macOS, Linux) with minimal setup. This is crucial when building tools that need to be distributed and used on different systems.

5. **Standard Library**: Go comes with a rich standard library, including robust support for file handling, networking, and more. It also provides packages like

flag for parsing command-line arguments and os/exec for running external commands, making it an ideal fit for building CLI tools.

6. **Lightweight and Easy Deployment**: Since Go compiles to a single static binary, there's no need for dependencies or additional runtime environments. This makes Go-based CLI tools easy to distribute and deploy.

Parsing Command-Line Arguments

One of the first steps when building a CLI application is to handle command-line arguments. Go provides several libraries to make this task easy, but the most commonly used is the flag package from the standard library.

1. The flag Package

The flag package allows you to define flags (also called command-line arguments) that users can provide when running your tool. Each flag has a name, a default value, and a description. It also handles parsing the flags when the program starts.

Let's start with a simple example of a CLI program that accepts a few command-line arguments:

Example: Basic Command-Line Tool with Flags

go
CopyEdit
```
package main

import (
        "flag"
        "fmt"
)
```

```go
func main() {
    // Define flags
    name := flag.String("name", "John Doe", "Your name")
    age := flag.Int("age", 30, "Your age")
    country := flag.String("country", "USA", "Your country")

    // Parse the flags
    flag.Parse()

    // Print the values
    fmt.Println("Hello,", *name)
    fmt.Println("Age:", *age)
    fmt.Println("Country:", *country)
}
```

Explanation:

- flag.String defines a flag named name with a default value of "John Doe", a description "Your name", and it stores the value in the variable name.
- flag.Int defines an integer flag named age with a default value of 30.
- flag.Parse() processes the command-line arguments and assigns the appropriate values to the variables.

Running the Program:

bash
CopyEdit
```
$ go run main.go --name "Alice" --age 25 --country "Canada"
Hello, Alice
```

Age: 25
Country: Canada

Output:

makefile
CopyEdit
Hello, Alice
Age: 25
Country: Canada

2. Handling Boolean Flags

Boolean flags are another common type of argument. These flags don't require a value—just their presence or absence determines their value.

Example: Boolean Flag

go
CopyEdit
```go
package main

import (
    "flag"
    "fmt"
)

func main() {
    // Define a boolean flag
    debug := flag.Bool("debug", false, "Enable debug mode")
```

```go
// Parse the flags
flag.Parse()

if *debug {
        fmt.Println("Debug mode enabled.")
} else {
        fmt.Println("Debug mode disabled.")

}

}
```

Explanation:

- flag.Bool defines a boolean flag named debug with a default value of false.
- The value of debug is checked and prints a message based on whether the flag was passed or not.

Running the Program:

bash
CopyEdit

```bash
$ go run main.go --debug
Debug mode enabled.
```

Building a More Complex CLI Tool

Let's build a more sophisticated CLI tool that can perform multiple operations, such as adding and listing items. In this example, we'll create a basic to-do list manager.

Example: Simple To-Do List CLI Tool

go

CopyEdit

```go
package main

import (
        "flag"
        "fmt"
        "os"
)

type ToDo struct {
        ID   int
        Task string
}

var toDoList []ToDo
var nextID int

func listTasks() {
        if len(toDoList) == 0 {
                fmt.Println("No tasks to display.")
                return
        }
        for _, task := range toDoList {
                fmt.Printf("ID: %d, Task: %s\n", task.ID, task.Task)
        }
}
```

```go
func addTask(task string) {
    toDoList = append(toDoList, ToDo{ID: nextID, Task: task})
    nextID++
    fmt.Printf("Task added: %s\n", task)
}


func main() {
    // Define flags
    action := flag.String("action", "", "Action to perform (add/list)")
    task := flag.String("task", "", "Task description (required for add)")

    // Parse the flags
    flag.Parse()

    if *action == "" {
        fmt.Println("Action is required. Use --action to specify 'add' or 'list'.")
        os.Exit(1)
    }

    switch *action {
    case "list":
        listTasks()
    case "add":
        if *task == "" {
            fmt.Println("You must provide a task description with --task.")
            os.Exit(1)
        }
        addTask(*task)
    default:
```

```
        fmt.Println("Invalid action. Use 'add' or 'list'.")
    }
}
```

Explanation:

- The ToDo struct represents a task with an ID and Task description.
- The addTask function adds a new task to the list.
- The listTasks function displays all tasks in the list.
- The main function handles the command-line arguments, checks for the required actions (add or list), and performs the appropriate operations.

Running the Program:

Adding a Task:

bash

CopyEdit

```
$ go run main.go --action add --task "Learn Go"
Task added: Learn Go
```

Listing Tasks:

bash

CopyEdit

```
$ go run main.go --action list
ID: 0, Task: Learn Go
```

Best Practices for Building CLI Tools in Go

1. **Organize Code into Functions**: As you build your CLI application, keep your code clean by organizing it into functions (like listTasks, addTask, etc.). This makes your code modular and easy to maintain.

265

2. **Provide Helpful Error Messages**: Always validate user input and provide helpful error messages if something goes wrong. This improves the user experience.

3. **Use Subcommands for Complex Tools**: For more advanced CLI tools, consider breaking your tool into subcommands. The flag package supports this with a combination of custom flags and argument parsing.

4. **Handle Exit Codes**: When a command-line application exits, it should use exit codes to indicate success or failure. Go allows you to use os.Exit() to set the exit code.

5. **Cross-Platform Compatibility**: Ensure that your CLI tool works on all major platforms. Test your application on Windows, macOS, and Linux to ensure it functions as expected across environments.

Building command-line tools in Go is a simple yet powerful way to create useful utilities. With Go's clean syntax, fast performance, and excellent library support, you can build reliable and efficient CLI applications. In this chapter, we explored how to parse command-line arguments and build a simple to-do list manager, demonstrating Go's capabilities for CLI development.

In this section, we will continue to explore building CLI tools in Go by diving into reading user input, using external libraries like cobra and flag, and building a simple to-do list CLI application that will leverage these techniques.

Reading User Input in Go

In many CLI tools, you need to interact with users by reading their input dynamically. Go makes it easy to do this using several built-in methods. Let's go over the most common ways to handle user input.

1. Using fmt.Scanln and fmt.Scanf

Go provides fmt.Scanln and fmt.Scanf for reading input from the user via the terminal.

- fmt.Scanln reads a line of input and assigns it to variables.
- fmt.Scanf is similar but offers more control over formatting.

Example: Using fmt.Scanln to Read User Input

go

CopyEdit

```go
package main

import (
        "fmt"
)

func main() {
        var name string
        fmt.Print("Enter your name: ")
```

```go
    _, err := fmt.Scanln(&name)

    if err != nil {

        fmt.Println("Error reading input:", err)

        return

    }

    fmt.Printf("Hello, %s!\n", name)

}
```

Explanation:

- fmt.Scanln(&name) reads a line of input from the terminal and assigns it to the name variable.
- The fmt.Printf function is then used to print a greeting with the user's input.

Running the Program:

bash

CopyEdit

```
$ go run main.go

Enter your name: Alice

Hello, Alice!
```

2. Using bufio.Reader for More Complex Input

For more complex input handling, like reading multi-line input or managing special characters, you can use bufio.Reader. This is a flexible way to read from the console.

Example: Using bufio.Reader for Input

go

CopyEdit

```go
package main

import (
        "bufio"
        "fmt"
        "os"
)

func main() {
        reader := bufio.NewReader(os.Stdin)
        fmt.Print("Enter a task description: ")
        task, _ := reader.ReadString('\n')
        fmt.Printf("You entered: %s", task)
```

```
}
```

Explanation:

- bufio.NewReader creates a reader to read from os.Stdin (standard input).
- reader.ReadString('\n') reads input until the user hits Enter.

Using External Libraries: cobra and flag

While the flag package in Go is great for basic command-line argument parsing, more complex applications often benefit from using external libraries like **Cobra**. Cobra simplifies the development of CLI applications by offering a framework for creating commands and subcommands, argument parsing, and more.

1. The flag Package (A Quick Recap)

The flag package allows you to define flags and arguments for your application. You saw this earlier in the simple to-do list CLI example. It's great for straightforward applications.

Example with flag (Quick Recap)

go

CopyEdit

```
package main

import (
```

```go
    "flag"

    "fmt"

)

func main() {

    // Define a flag

    task := flag.String("task", "", "Task description")

    flag.Parse()

    if *task == "" {

            fmt.Println("Please provide a task with --task")

    } else {

            fmt.Printf("Task: %s\n", *task)

    }

}
```

---

2. The cobra Package

Cobra is a widely used library for building modern CLI tools in Go. It allows you to easily create commands, subcommands, and handle flag parsing.

Installing Cobra

To get started with Cobra, you'll need to install it:

bash

CopyEdit

```
go get -u github.com/spf13/cobra@latest
```

Creating a Simple CLI App with Cobra

Let's now enhance the to-do list CLI app by incorporating Cobra. This will give us the ability to add subcommands, flags, and improve the user experience.

go

CopyEdit

```go
package main

import (

    "fmt"

    "github.com/spf13/cobra"

)


var toDoList []string


// Add a task

var addCmd = &cobra.Command{

    Use:   "add",
```

```go
        Short: "Add a task to the to-do list",

        Run: func(cmd *cobra.Command, args []string) {

                if len(args) < 1 {

                        fmt.Println("Please provide a task description")

                        return

                }

                task := args[0]

                toDoList = append(toDoList, task)

                fmt.Printf("Task '%s' added to the to-do list\n", task)

        },

}


// List all tasks

var listCmd = &cobra.Command{

        Use:   "list",

        Short: "List all tasks in the to-do list",

        Run: func(cmd *cobra.Command, args []string) {

                if len(toDoList) == 0 {

                        fmt.Println("No tasks to display.")
```

```go
			return

		}

/		fmt.Println("To-Do List:")

		for _, task := range toDoList {

			fmt.Println(task)

		}

	},

}


func main() {

	var rootCmd = &cobra.Command{Use: "todo"}


	// Add subcommands to root command

	rootCmd.AddCommand(addCmd, listCmd)


	// Execute the root command

	if err := rootCmd.Execute(); err != nil {

		fmt.Println(err)

	}
```

}

Explanation:

- addCmd and listCmd are two subcommands that allow users to add tasks and list all tasks.
- rootCmd.AddCommand(addCmd, listCmd) links the subcommands to the root command.
- The main function initializes the root command and runs it.

Running the Program:

Adding a Task:

bash

CopyEdit

```
$ go run main.go add "Learn Go"
```

Task 'Learn Go' added to the to-do list

1. **Listing Tasks:**

   bash

   CopyEdit

   ```
   $ go run main.go list
   ```

To-Do List:

Learn Go

Building a Simple To-Do List CLI Application

In this section, we've already touched on building a simple to-do list CLI tool using both the flag and cobra libraries. Let's now create a fully functional to-do list CLI app that allows users to add, list, and remove tasks.

Enhancing the To-Do List App with Cobra

go

CopyEdit

```go
package main

import (
        "fmt"

        "github.com/spf13/cobra"

        "os"
)


var toDoList []string


// Add a task

var addCmd = &cobra.Command{
```

```go
    Use:   "add",

    Short: "Add a task to the to-do list",

    Run: func(cmd *cobra.Command, args []string) {

        if len(args) < 1 {

            fmt.Println("Please provide a task description")

            return

        }

        task := args[0]

        toDoList = append(toDoList, task)

        fmt.Printf("Task '%s' added to the to-do list\n", task)

    },

}


// List all tasks

var listCmd = &cobra.Command{

    Use:   "list",

    Short: "List all tasks in the to-do list",

    Run: func(cmd *cobra.Command, args []string) {

        if len(toDoList) == 0 {
```

```go
                        fmt.Println("No tasks to display.")

                        return

                }

                fmt.Println("To-Do List:")

                for _, task := range toDoList {

                        fmt.Println(task)

                }

        },

}



// Remove a task

var removeCmd = &cobra.Command{

        Use:   "remove",

        Short: "Remove a task from the to-do list",

        Run: func(cmd *cobra.Command, args []string) {

                if len(args) < 1 {

                        fmt.Println("Please provide a task ID to remove")

                        return

                }
```

```go
        taskID := args[0]

        var newList []string

        for i, task := range toDoList {

            if fmt.Sprintf("%d", i) == taskID {

                fmt.Printf("Removing task: %s\n", task)

            } else {

                newList = append(newList, task)

            }

        }

        toDoList = newList

    },
}


func main() {

    var rootCmd = &cobra.Command{Use: "todo"}


    // Add subcommands to root command

    rootCmd.AddCommand(addCmd, listCmd, removeCMD)
```

```
// Execute the root command

if err := rootCmd.Execute(); err != nil {

        fmt.Println(err)

        os.Exit(1)

    }

}
```

Features:

- **Add Task:** Adds a new task to the to-do list.
- **List Tasks:** Lists all tasks in the to-do list.
- **Remove Task:** Removes a task from the to-do list by its ID.

Running the App

Add a Task:

bash

CopyEdit

$ go run main.go add "Finish Go book"

Task 'Finish Go book' added to the to-do list

List All Tasks:

bash

CopyEdit

$ go run main.go list

To-Do List:

Remove a Task:

bash

CopyEdit

$ go run main.go remove 0

Removing task: Finish Go book

In this section, we've learned how to enhance our CLI applications by reading user input effectively and using external libraries like flag and cobra. You saw how to structure a more complex CLI tool by allowing for multiple commands (add, list, remove). The Cobra library, in particular, is excellent for scaling up your CLI applications, providing you with a way to manage commands and flags easily.

These skills will be crucial as you continue to build more advanced command-line tools and enhance your development process.

Chapter 11: Web Development with Go: Creating REST APIs

In this chapter, we will explore how Go can be used to build web applications, particularly focusing on creating RESTful APIs. We'll cover the basics of web development with Go, how the net/http package works, and the key components of building a simple REST API.

Introduction to Web Development in Go

Go is a powerful and efficient language for web development, especially for building scalable and fast web services. While Go might not have as many web frameworks as other languages, its simplicity, performance, and built-in support for concurrency make it an excellent choice for developing web APIs and microservices.

Go's web development capabilities are primarily provided by the standard library, particularly the net/http package. This allows you to create HTTP servers, handle requests, and serve responses without the need for third-party frameworks.

Understanding the net/http Package

The net/http package in Go provides all the necessary tools to handle HTTP requests and responses. Let's look at the basics of the package and how you can use it to set up a simple web server.

1. Basic HTTP Server with net/http

A basic Go web server can be set up with just a few lines of code using the net/http package. The server listens for incoming HTTP requests, and you can define handlers to process those requests.

Here's a simple example of a basic web server in Go:

```go
CopyEdit
package main

import (
        "fmt"
        "net/http"
)

func handler(w http.ResponseWriter, r *http.Request) {
        fmt.Fprintf(w, "Hello, world!")
}

func main() {
        http.HandleFunc("/", handler) // Register handler for root URL
        fmt.Println("Server is running on http://localhost:8080")
        http.ListenAndServe(":8080", nil) // Start server on port 8080
}
```

Explanation:

- http.HandleFunc("/", handler) registers a route ("/") and a handler function (handler), which handles all incoming requests to the root URL.
- http.ListenAndServe(":8080", nil) starts an HTTP server listening on port 8080.

Running the Program:

bash

CopyEdit

```
$ go run main.go
Server is running on http://localhost:8080
```

Now, open your browser and navigate to http://localhost:8080. You should see the response: "Hello, world!".

---

2. Handling HTTP Requests

In Go, HTTP handlers are functions that accept two parameters:

- http.ResponseWriter: Used to construct the HTTP response.
- *http.Request: Contains the details of the incoming HTTP request, such as method, headers, body, and URL.

Here's an example of how to handle a GET request with query parameters:

go

CopyEdit

```
package main

import (
```

```go
    "fmt"
    "net/http"
)


func greetHandler(w http.ResponseWriter, r *http.Request) {
    name := r.URL.Query().Get("name") // Get the 'name' query parameter
    if name == "" {
        name = "Guest"
    }
    fmt.Fprintf(w, "Hello, %s!", name)
}


func main() {
    http.HandleFunc("/greet", greetHandler)
    http.ListenAndServe(":8080", nil)
}
```

Explanation:

- r.URL.Query().Get("name") retrieves the value of the query parameter name from the URL (e.g., /greet?name=Alice).
- If no name parameter is provided, it defaults to "Guest".

Test the Program:

Start the server, then open your browser and test it:

- http://localhost:8080/greet?name=John returns "Hello, John!"
- http://localhost:8080/greet returns "Hello, Guest!"

Creating REST APIs with Go

A RESTful API is an architectural style for providing standards-based communication between clients and servers. It typically involves creating endpoints that support the basic HTTP methods such as GET, POST, PUT, and DELETE.

1. Creating a Simple REST API

Let's now build a simple REST API for managing a to-do list. This API will allow users to create, read, update, and delete tasks using standard HTTP methods.

go
CopyEdit
```go
package main

import (
        "encoding/json"
        "fmt"
        "net/http"
        "sync"
)

type Task struct {
        ID          int    `json:"id"`
        Description string `json:"description"`
}

var tasks = []Task{}
var nextID = 1
var mu sync.Mutex
```

```go
// Get all tasks
func getTasksHandler(w http.ResponseWriter, r *http.Request) {
        mu.Lock()
        defer mu.Unlock()

        w.Header().Set("Content-Type", "application/json")
        json.NewEncoder(w).Encode(tasks)
}


// Create a new task
func createTaskHandler(w http.ResponseWriter, r *http.Request) {
        mu.Lock()
        defer mu.Unlock()

        var task Task
        if err := json.NewDecoder(r.Body).Decode(&task); err != nil {
                http.Error(w, err.Error(), http.StatusBadRequest)
                return
        }

        task.ID = nextID
        nextID++
        tasks = append(tasks, task)

        w.Header().Set("Content-Type", "application/json")
        w.WriteHeader(http.StatusCreated)
        json.NewEncoder(w).Encode(task)
}
```

```go
// Delete a task by ID
func deleteTaskHandler(w http.ResponseWriter, r *http.Request) {
    mu.Lock()
    defer mu.Unlock()

    // Parse the ID from the URL
    id := r.URL.Query().Get("id")
    if id == "" {
        http.Error(w, "ID is required", http.StatusBadRequest)
        return
    }

    for i, task := range tasks {
        if fmt.Sprintf("%d", task.ID) == id {
            tasks = append(tasks[:i], tasks[i+1:]...)
            w.WriteHeader(http.StatusNoContent) // 204 No Content
            return
        }
    }

    http.Error(w, "Task not found", http.StatusNotFound)
}

func main() {
    http.HandleFunc("/tasks", getTasksHandler)
    http.HandleFunc("/tasks/create", createTaskHandler)
    http.HandleFunc("/tasks/delete", deleteTaskHandler)

    fmt.Println("Server running at http://localhost:8080")
```

```
http.ListenAndServe(":8080", nil)
}
```

Explanation:

- We define a Task struct with ID and Description fields.
- The getTasksHandler function handles GET requests to /tasks to return all tasks.
- The createTaskHandler function handles POST requests to /tasks/create to add a new task.
- The deleteTaskHandler function handles DELETE requests to /tasks/delete?id=1 to delete a task by its ID.
- The sync.Mutex ensures thread-safe access to the tasks slice.

Testing the REST API:

GET /tasks: Returns all tasks in JSON format.

bash

CopyEdit

```
$ curl http://localhost:8080/tasks
```

- **POST /tasks/create**: Adds a new task. You can test it using a tool like Postman or curl.

  bash

  CopyEdit

  ```
  $ curl -X POST -d '{"description": "Learn Go"}' -H "Content-Type: application/json" http://localhost:8080/tasks/create
  ```

- **DELETE /tasks/delete?id=1**: Deletes a task by its ID.

  bash

  CopyEdit

  ```
  $ curl -X DELETE "http://localhost:8080/tasks/delete?id=1"
  ```

We introduced the basics of web development in Go, focusing on how to create a simple REST API using Go's net/http package. You learned how to set up a basic web server, handle HTTP requests, and implement CRUD (Create, Read, Update, Delete) operations for managing data.

Go's built-in tools like net/http and json make it an excellent choice for building fast, efficient web services. By mastering these concepts, you'll be well-equipped to develop REST APIs, microservices, and web applications in Go.

Handling HTTP Requests and Responses

In Go, HTTP requests and responses are fundamental to web development. The net/http package provides a straightforward way to handle HTTP requests, process them, and generate responses. Understanding how to work with HTTP requests and responses is essential for building any web application.

1. HTTP Request Handling

When an HTTP request is made to your server, Go's http.Request type provides all the information you need to handle that request. This includes details about the HTTP method (GET, POST, PUT, DELETE), URL parameters, headers, and the request body.

Here's an overview of common operations when handling HTTP requests:

- **Getting URL Parameters**: You can retrieve query parameters from the URL using the URL.Query() method.
- **Reading Request Body**: Use r.Body to access the data sent in the request body, commonly used for POST and PUT requests.
- **Reading Headers**: You can access the request headers using r.Header.

Example of Handling HTTP Requests

Let's say we need to handle a POST request where the client sends data in JSON format. The data could be a task description to add to a task list.

go

CopyEdit

```go
package main

import (

    "encoding/json"

    "fmt"

    "net/http"

)


type Task struct {

    ID          int    `json:"id"`

    Description string `json:"description"`

}


var tasks []Task

var nextID int
```

```go
// Create a new task

func createTaskHandler(w http.ResponseWriter, r *http.Request) {

    var newTask Task


    // Read the incoming JSON request body

    if err := json.NewDecoder(r.Body).Decode(&newTask); err != nil {

        http.Error(w, err.Error(), http.StatusBadRequest)

        return

    }


    // Assign an ID to the new task and increment nextID

    newTask.ID = nextID

    nextID++


    // Add the new task to the tasks list

    tasks = append(tasks, newTask)


    // Respond with the created task in JSON format
```

```
    w.Header().Set("Content-Type", "application/json")

    w.WriteHeader(http.StatusCreated)

    json.NewEncoder(w).Encode(newTask)

}

func main() {

    http.HandleFunc("/tasks/create", createTaskHandler)

    http.ListenAndServe(":8080", nil)

}
```

Explanation:

- json.NewDecoder(r.Body).Decode(&newTask) reads and decodes the JSON body from the request into the Task struct.
- After creating the new task, the server sends a response back to the client in JSON format using json.NewEncoder(w).Encode(newTask).

Testing the POST Request:

You can test this endpoint using a tool like Postman or curl. Here's an example using curl:

bash

CopyEdit

```
$ curl -X POST -d '{"description": "Learn Go"}' -H "Content-Type: application/json" http://localhost:8080/tasks/create
```

This request will create a new task with the description "Learn Go". The server will respond with the newly created task in JSON format.

Creating a Simple REST API in Go

In this section, we'll expand on the basic server example to create a simple REST API that allows users to manage a to-do list. The REST API will support the following operations:

1. **GET**: Retrieve all tasks.
2. **POST**: Create a new task.
3. **PUT**: Update an existing task.
4. **DELETE**: Remove a task.

1. Defining the Task Structure

To start, we need to define the Task struct, which represents each task in our to-do list. Each task will have:

- ID: A unique identifier for the task.
- Description: A description of the task.

Here's a basic struct for a task:

go

CopyEdit

```
type Task struct {
```

```go
    ID          int    `json:"id"`

    Description string `json:"description"`

}
```

2. Setting Up Routes and Handlers

Now that we have the basic structure, let's set up the routes and handlers for our REST API.

go

CopyEdit

```go
package main


import (

        "encoding/json"

        "fmt"

        "net/http"

        "sync"

)



var tasks []Task
```

```go
var nextID int

var mu sync.Mutex


// Get all tasks

func getTasksHandler(w http.ResponseWriter, r *http.Request) {

    mu.Lock()

    defer mu.Unlock()


    w.Header().Set("Content-Type", "application/json")

    json.NewEncoder(w).Encode(tasks)

}


// Create a new task

func createTaskHandler(w http.ResponseWriter, r *http.Request) {

    mu.Lock()

    defer mu.Unlock()


    var task Task

    if err := json.NewDecoder(r.Body).Decode(&task); err != nil {
```

```go
        http.Error(w, err.Error(), http.StatusBadRequest)

        return

    }


    task.ID = nextID

    nextID++

    tasks = append(tasks, task)


    w.Header().Set("Content-Type", "application/json")

    w.WriteHeader(http.StatusCreated)

    json.NewEncoder(w).Encode(task)

}


// Delete a task by ID

func deleteTaskHandler(w http.ResponseWriter, r *http.Request) {

    mu.Lock()

    defer mu.Unlock()


    id := r.URL.Query().Get("id")
```

```go
        if id == "" {

                http.Error(w, "ID is required", http.StatusBadRequest)

                return

        }


        for i, task := range tasks {

                if fmt.Sprintf("%d", task.ID) == id {

                        tasks = append(tasks[:i], tasks[i+1:]...)

                        w.WriteHeader(http.StatusNoContent) // 204 No Content

                        return

                }

        }


        http.Error(w, "Task not found", http.StatusNotFound)

}


func main() {

        http.HandleFunc("/tasks", getTasksHandler)

        http.HandleFunc("/tasks/create", createTaskHandler)
```

```
http.HandleFunc("/tasks/delete", deleteTaskHandler)



fmt.Println("Server running at http://localhost:8080")

http.ListenAndServe(":8080", nil)
}
```

Explanation:

- getTasksHandler: Handles GET requests and returns all tasks in the list.
- createTaskHandler: Handles POST requests and creates a new task.
- deleteTaskHandler: Handles DELETE requests, removing a task by its ID.

3. Implementing CRUD Operations

Now, let's break down the CRUD operations in our API.

- **GET /tasks**: This route retrieves all the tasks in the list. It uses the json.NewEncoder(w).Encode(tasks) to send the task data as a JSON response.
- **POST /tasks/create**: This route allows a user to create a new task. The client sends the task data in the request body, which the server decodes and appends to the task list.
- **DELETE /tasks/delete?id=1**: This route removes a task with the given ID from the list. The task ID is passed as a query parameter (id).

Implementing CRUD Operations

The key to REST APIs is their ability to perform CRUD operations. Let's ensure that our API supports all four CRUD operations: Create, Read, Update, and Delete.

Create:

This was implemented with the createTaskHandler function, which listens for POST requests on /tasks/create. It reads the task description from the request body, assigns an ID to the new task, and appends it to the tasks list.

Read:

The getTasksHandler function handles GET requests to /tasks. It retrieves all tasks and sends them back as a JSON response.

Delete:

The deleteTaskHandler function listens for DELETE requests to /tasks/delete. It removes a task from the list based on the provided id query parameter.

Update:

While not included in the current example, you can add a PUT method to update tasks. The PUT method would involve receiving a task ID and updated task data, replacing the old task with the new one.

Testing the API

You can test the API using tools like curl or Postman.

GET /tasks: Retrieve all tasks.

bash

CopyEdit

```
$ curl http://localhost:8080/tasks
```

- **POST /tasks/create**: Add a new task.

  bash

  CopyEdit

  ```
  $ curl -X POST -d '{"description": "Learn Go"}' -H "Content-Type: application/json" http://localhost:8080/tasks/create
  ```

- **DELETE /tasks/delete?id=1**: Delete a task by ID.

  bash

  CopyEdit

  ```
  $ curl -X DELETE "http://localhost:8080/tasks/delete?id=1"
  ```

In this section, you learned how to build a simple REST API using Go. We walked through how to handle HTTP requests, manage data, and implement CRUD operations. The example we built, a basic to-do list API, showcases how Go can be used to handle web requests efficiently and with minimal overhead.

Go's built-in support for handling HTTP requests and responses makes it a great choice for building RESTful APIs. You now have a foundation to expand this example, adding more functionality and improving the system based on your needs. Whether you're building a small service or a large-scale application, Go's simplicity, speed, and concurrency support make it a powerful tool for web development.

Middleware in Go: Logging, Authentication, and More

Middleware in Go is a powerful way to manage tasks that need to be performed before or after the request is processed by your handler. Middleware is essentially a function that wraps around your HTTP request handler, allowing you to add functionality such as logging, authentication, input validation, and more, without modifying the actual request handlers.

1. What is Middleware?

Middleware is a function that can intercept requests coming into your web server. It can modify the request, process it, log details, or even reject it before it reaches the main handler. Middleware functions are executed in the order they are added to the HTTP request pipeline.

Go's http.HandleFunc() does not have built-in support for middleware, but you can easily create your own middleware by creating a function that takes an http.Handler and returns an http.Handler.

2. Creating Middleware

A simple middleware function might look like this:

go

CopyEdit

```
package main


import (

    "fmt"
```

```go
    "net/http"

)


// Middleware that logs each incoming request

func loggingMiddleware(next http.Handler) http.Handler {

    return http.HandlerFunc(func(w http.ResponseWriter, r *http.Request) {

        fmt.Printf("Received request: %s %s\n", r.Method, r.URL.Path)

        next.ServeHTTP(w, r)

    })

}
```

In this example, the loggingMiddleware function prints each incoming request to the console before passing the request to the actual handler. You can chain multiple middlewares to handle various tasks.

3. Authentication Middleware

A common use of middleware is to handle authentication. Let's say we want to add a middleware function that checks if a user is authenticated before allowing access to a protected route.

go

CopyEdit

```go
// Middleware that checks if the user is authenticated

func authenticationMiddleware(next http.Handler) http.Handler {

    return http.HandlerFunc(func(w http.ResponseWriter, r *http.Request) {

        authHeader := r.Header.Get("Authorization")

        if authHeader == "" {

            http.Error(w, "Unauthorized", http.StatusUnauthorized)

            return

        }

        // Optionally, add further validation logic for token verification

        // For now, we simply allow any non-empty token

        next.ServeHTTP(w, r)

    })

}
```

This middleware checks the Authorization header of the request. If it's empty or missing, the server responds with a 401 Unauthorized status.

4. Applying Middleware

To use middleware in your Go application, wrap the handler with the middleware function. Here's an example of applying both the logging and authentication middleware:

go

CopyEdit

```go
func main() {

    http.HandleFunc("/protected", func(w http.ResponseWriter, r *http.Request) {

        fmt.Fprintf(w, "You have access to the protected resource!")

    })

    // Apply middleware

    http.Handle("/protected",
loggingMiddleware(authenticationMiddleware(http.HandlerFunc(protectedHandler))))

    http.ListenAndServe(":8080", nil)

}
```

In this example, both loggingMiddleware and authenticationMiddleware are applied to the /protected route.

Connecting Go to a Database (PostgreSQL/MySQL)

Databases are a core part of many web applications, and Go makes it easy to connect to and interact with both PostgreSQL and MySQL databases. In this section, we will look at how to connect to a database, perform basic operations (such as querying and inserting data), and work with database drivers.

1. Setting Up PostgreSQL

For PostgreSQL, we will use the github.com/lib/pq package, which is a pure Go driver for PostgreSQL.

To install the PostgreSQL driver, run:

bash

CopyEdit

```
go get github.com/lib/pq
```

Once the driver is installed, you can use it to connect to your PostgreSQL database.

2. Example: Connecting to PostgreSQL

Here's how you can connect to a PostgreSQL database in Go:

go

CopyEdit

```
package main

import (
    "database/sql"

    "fmt"

    "log"
```

```go
        _ "github.com/lib/pq"

)


const (

        // Database connection details

        host     = "localhost"

        port     = 5432

        user     = "postgres"

        password = "password"

        dbname   = "mydb"

)


func main() {

        // Connection string for PostgreSQL

        psqlInfo := fmt.Sprintf("host=%s port=%d user=%s password=%s dbname=%s
sslmode=disable", host, port, user, password, dbname)


        // Open a connection to the database
```

```go
db, err := sql.Open("postgres", psqlInfo)

if err != nil {

        log.Fatal("Error opening database: ", err)

}

defer db.Close()


// Test the connection

err = db.Ping()

if err != nil {

        log.Fatal("Error connecting to database: ", err)

}


fmt.Println("Successfully connected to PostgreSQL!")

}
```

Explanation:

- The sql.Open() function establishes a connection to the database using the connection string.
- db.Ping() ensures that the connection is valid.

- Ensure that PostgreSQL is running and that the credentials (host, port, user, password) match those of your PostgreSQL server.

3. Performing CRUD Operations with PostgreSQL

Once connected to the database, you can perform CRUD operations. Here's an example of inserting data into a PostgreSQL database.

go

CopyEdit

```
func insertTask(db *sql.DB, description string) (int, error) {

    // SQL query to insert a new task into the database

    query := `INSERT INTO tasks (description) VALUES ($1) RETURNING id`

    var id int

    err := db.QueryRow(query, description).Scan(&id)

    if err != nil {

        return 0, err

    }

    return id, nil

}
```

In this example, we are inserting a new task into the tasks table and returning the id of the newly inserted task.

309

4. Querying Data from PostgreSQL

You can retrieve data from your database using the Query() method. Here's how you can retrieve all tasks from the tasks table:

go

CopyEdit

```go
func getTasks(db *sql.DB) ([]Task, error) {

    rows, err := db.Query("SELECT id, description FROM tasks")

    if err != nil {

        return nil, err

    }

    defer rows.Close()


    var tasks []Task

    for rows.Next() {

        var task Task

        if err := rows.Scan(&task.ID, &task.Description); err != nil {

            return nil, err

        }

        tasks = append(tasks, task)
```

```
        }

        return tasks, nil

}
```

Here, the rows.Scan() method maps the values from the database rows into the Task struct.

5. Setting Up MySQL

For MySQL, we will use the github.com/go-sql-driver/mysql package, which is a MySQL driver for Go.

To install the MySQL driver, run:

bash

CopyEdit

go get github.com/go-sql-driver/mysql

Once the driver is installed, you can connect to MySQL just as you did with PostgreSQL.

6. Example: Connecting to MySQL

Here's how you can connect to a MySQL database:

go

CopyEdit

package main

```go
import (

    "database/sql"

    "fmt"

    "log"


    _ "github.com/go-sql-driver/mysql"

)


func main() {

    // Set up MySQL connection string

    dsn := "root:password@tcp(localhost:3306)/mydb"


    // Open connection to the database

    db, err := sql.Open("mysql", dsn)

    if err != nil {

        log.Fatal("Error opening database: ", err)

    }

    defer db.Close()
```

```
// Test the connection

if err := db.Ping(); err != nil {

        log.Fatal("Error connecting to database: ", err)

}


fmt.Println("Successfully connected to MySQL!")

}
```

The setup is almost identical to PostgreSQL, except for the connection string format.

7. Performing CRUD Operations with MySQL

You can insert, update, and query data in MySQL just as you did with PostgreSQL. The syntax for interacting with MySQL is the same, except for the specific SQL dialect for MySQL.

In this section, we covered how to use middleware in Go to add functionality like logging and authentication to your web applications. We also learned how to connect to PostgreSQL and MySQL databases, perform CRUD operations, and work with databases in Go.

Middleware is an essential concept for managing tasks that need to run before or after processing a request, while database connections enable your applications to interact

with persistent data. Whether you're building a simple application or a complex web service, Go provides the tools you need to handle these tasks efficiently.

Chapter 12: Testing and Debugging in Go

Why Testing Matters in Software Development

Testing is a fundamental part of the software development process that ensures your code is correct, reliable, and behaves as expected. Without testing, your application may silently fail under specific conditions, causing bugs that are difficult to track down.

1. The Importance of Testing in Go

Go embraces testing as an essential part of its development ecosystem. It provides built-in support for unit testing, benchmarking, and performance testing, making it easy for developers to write comprehensive tests. This reduces the likelihood of defects and ensures that your codebase remains maintainable, even as it grows.

By having automated tests in place, developers can:

- **Catch Bugs Early**: With unit tests and integration tests, bugs can be identified early in the development process before they affect production.
- **Increase Code Quality**: Tests improve the reliability and stability of your code.
- **Maintain Confidence**: Testing allows developers to make changes or refactor code with confidence, knowing that tests will catch unintended side effects.
- **Document Behavior**: Tests act as documentation for your code's behavior, making it easier for other developers to understand how the code works.

Writing Unit Tests in Go

Unit testing in Go is simple and straightforward. The language provides the testing package, which contains all the necessary tools to write and run tests.

1. Setting Up Test Files

In Go, test files are conventionally named with the suffix _test.go (for example, main_test.go or calculator_test.go). These files contain your test functions.

Here is an example of a basic unit test:

```go
CopyEdit
package main

import "testing"

// Function to be tested
func Add(a, b int) int {
    return a + b
}

// Unit test for the Add function
func TestAdd(t *testing.T) {
    result := Add(2, 3)
    expected := 5

    if result != expected {
        t.Errorf("Add(2, 3) = %d; want %d", result, expected)
    }
```

}

- **The TestXxx Function**: Go test functions always start with the Test prefix, followed by the name of the function being tested (e.g., TestAdd for the Add function).
- **The t *testing.T Argument**: This argument allows you to report errors, log information, and control test execution. Use t.Errorf or t.Fatal to log errors or failure messages.
- **Testing Functionality**: In the TestAdd function, we test if the Add function works as expected by comparing its result with the expected value. If it doesn't match, we use t.Errorf to indicate a failure.

2. Running Tests

To run the tests in your Go project, use the go test command:

bash

CopyEdit

```
go test
```

By default, go test will search for all test files (_test.go files) in the current directory, run the tests, and report the results.

If your project has multiple test files, you can run tests from a specific file:

bash

CopyEdit

```
go test -v calculator_test.go
```

The -v flag makes the test output more verbose, showing which tests passed or failed.

317

3. Testing Multiple Cases with Subtests

You can also run multiple tests within a single test function using subtests. This is helpful when you want to test the same function with different inputs.

go
CopyEdit
```go
func TestAdd(t *testing.T) {
    tests := []struct {
        a, b     int
        expected int
    }{
        {2, 3, 5},
        {5, 7, 12},
        {-1, 1, 0},
    }

    for _, tt := range tests {
        t.Run(fmt.Sprintf("%d+%d", tt.a, tt.b), func(t *testing.T) {
            result := Add(tt.a, tt.b)
            if result != tt.expected {
                t.Errorf("Add(%d, %d) = %d; want %d", tt.a, tt.b, result, tt.expected)
            }
        })
    }
}
```

In this example:

- We create a slice of test cases that hold different inputs and expected outputs.

- We loop through each test case, running it as a subtest using t.Run().

4. Testing Edge Cases

Unit tests should cover edge cases to ensure your functions behave correctly under a variety of conditions.

For example, in the Add function, you might want to test:

- Adding zero.
- Adding negative numbers.
- Adding large numbers.

go
CopyEdit
```go
func TestAddEdgeCases(t *testing.T) {
    tests := []struct {
        a, b    int
        expected int
    }{
        {0, 0, 0},       // Adding zero
        {-1, 1, 0},      // Negative and positive numbers
        {int(^uint(0) >> 1), 1, int(^uint(0) >> 1) + 1}, // Large numbers (edge case)
    }

    for _, tt := range tests {
        t.Run(fmt.Sprintf("%d+%d", tt.a, tt.b), func(t *testing.T) {
            result := Add(tt.a, tt.b)
            if result != tt.expected {
                t.Errorf("Add(%d, %d) = %d; want %d", tt.a, tt.b, result, tt.expected)
            }
```

```
	})
  }
}
```

5. Table-Driven Tests

Table-driven tests are a Go idiom for writing tests with different input-output pairs. These tests allow you to easily add or modify test cases without having to change the structure of your test function. This is useful when you want to run a function with a variety of input values.

Debugging in Go

Debugging is the process of identifying and fixing bugs or issues in your program. Go provides several tools and techniques to help you debug your applications effectively.

1. Using Print Statements

The simplest form of debugging in Go is adding print statements to your code to inspect values during execution. You can use fmt.Println() to print out variable values, helping you trace the flow of the program.

go
CopyEdit

```go
fmt.Println("Debugging: value of x:", x)
```

2. The Go Debugger (GDB)

Go also integrates with popular debuggers like GDB (GNU Debugger). You can use GDB to pause your program at breakpoints, inspect variables, and step through the code to find issues.

To use GDB, build your Go program with debugging symbols:

bash

CopyEdit

```
go build -gcflags="all=-N -l"
```

Then, run the program in GDB:

bash

CopyEdit

```
gdb ./your_program
```

Within GDB, you can set breakpoints and step through your code using commands like break, next, step, and print.

3. The Delve Debugger

Delve is a powerful, Go-specific debugger that allows you to inspect and debug your Go programs.

To install Delve:

bash

CopyEdit

```
go install github.com/go-delve/delve/cmd/dlv@latest
```

To run Delve:

bash
CopyEdit
```
dlv debug
```

Once inside the Delve prompt, you can set breakpoints, examine variables, and control the flow of the program. Some common Delve commands include:

- break <function>: Set a breakpoint at the specified function.
- continue: Continue running the program until the next breakpoint.
- print <variable>: Print the value of a variable.

We covered the essential aspects of testing and debugging in Go. Testing is vital for ensuring the correctness and reliability of your application. We learned how to write unit tests, handle different test cases, and test edge cases effectively using Go's built-in testing package. Additionally, we explored tools for debugging Go applications, such as using print statements, GDB, and Delve, which help developers identify and fix issues in their code.

By incorporating testing and debugging into your development workflow, you will not only catch bugs early but also improve the overall quality and maintainability of your Go applications.

Understanding the testing and testify Packages

Go provides a robust built-in testing framework through the testing package, but for more advanced test features, the testify package is widely used. It adds more powerful assertions, mocking, and other utilities to make writing tests more flexible and concise.

---

1. The testing Package: Overview

The testing package is the standard Go testing package, and it provides basic functionality for writing and running tests. You use the testing.T struct to report errors in your test functions. While the testing package is sufficient for many use cases, it lacks some advanced features like custom assertions, mocks, and easier test organization.

Key Functions of the testing Package:

- **t.Errorf()**: Used to log errors when the test fails. The test continues to run.
- **t.Fatal()**: Logs the error and stops the execution of the test immediately.
- **t.Run()**: Creates subtests within a test function to run multiple test cases.

go

CopyEdit

```go
func TestAddition(t *testing.T) {

    t.Run("Positive Numbers", func(t *testing.T) {

        result := Add(1, 2)

        if result != 3 {
```

```
        t.Errorf("Expected 3 but got %d", result)

    }

})

}
```

The testing package works well for simple tests but lacks some of the advanced features found in other testing libraries like testify.

---

2. The testify Package: Enhancing Your Tests

testify is a popular third-party package in the Go ecosystem that enhances the built-in testing functionality. It provides more readable and powerful assertions, mocking, and other utilities that simplify writing tests.

You can install the testify package using:

bash

CopyEdit

```
go get github.com/stretchr/testify
```

The package includes several important features:

- **Assertions**: Simplifies comparisons and condition checking in tests.

- **Mocking**: Helps simulate and control dependencies, such as databases or APIs, to focus on testing business logic.
- **Suite**: Allows you to group tests into reusable test setups, making it easier to manage large test suites.

Commonly Used Testify Assertions:

- assert.Equal(): Checks if two values are equal.
- assert.NotNil(): Ensures a value is not nil.
- assert.Error(): Verifies that an error is returned.

Example of testify usage:

go

CopyEdit

```
package main

import (
    "testing"
    "github.com/stretchr/testify/assert"
)

func TestAdd(t *testing.T) {
    result := Add(2, 3)
```

```go
    assert.Equal(t, 5, result, "They should be equal!")

}
```

In this example, assert.Equal() compares the result of Add(2, 3) to 5, and if they are not equal, the test will fail with the message "They should be equal!".

Mocking with testify:

testify also includes a mocking framework that makes it easy to create mocks for interfaces. This is useful when testing functions that interact with external systems, like databases or APIs.

go

CopyEdit

```go
package main

import (

    "testing"

    "github.com/stretchr/testify/mock"

)


type Database interface {

    GetUser(id int) (string, error)
```

```go
}


type MockDatabase struct {

    mock.Mock

}


func (m *MockDatabase) GetUser(id int) (string, error) {

    args := m.Called(id)

    return args.String(0), args.Error(1)

}


func TestGetUser(t *testing.T) {

    mockDB := new(MockDatabase)

    mockDB.On("GetUser", 1).Return("John Doe", nil)


    user, err := mockDB.GetUser(1)


    assert.NoError(t, err)

    assert.Equal(t, "John Doe", user)
```

```
    mockDB.AssertExpectations(t)

}
```

In the example above:

- **Mocking the Database**: We create a mock version of the Database interface with testify/mock.
- **Defining Expectations**: The On() method sets up expectations for the mock's behavior. We expect that GetUser(1) will return "John Doe" and nil for the error.
- **Asserting Expectations**: AssertExpectations(t) ensures the mock methods were called as expected.

Writing Table-Driven Tests

Table-driven tests are a widely recommended Go testing pattern, especially when you need to run the same logic for multiple input-output pairs. Instead of writing multiple test cases manually, you define a table of test cases (a slice of structs) and loop through each case.

This approach helps to keep your tests clean, concise, and scalable.

1. Benefits of Table-Driven Tests

- **Simplified Tests**: Instead of writing similar tests for different inputs, you can use one test function to handle multiple cases.
- **Scalability**: It's easy to add more test cases, and you don't have to modify the test function.

- **Readability**: The structure is organized, and it's clear what inputs are being tested and what the expected outputs are.

2. Example of Table-Driven Tests

Let's apply this pattern to our Add function.

go

CopyEdit

```go
package main

import (

    "testing"

    "github.com/stretchr/testify/assert"

)


func TestAdd(t *testing.T) {

    testCases := []struct {

        a, b    int

        expected int

    }{

        {1, 2, 3},
```

```
    {2, 3, 5},

    {0, 0, 0},

    {-1, 1, 0},

    }


for _, tt := range testCases {

    t.Run(fmt.Sprintf("%d+%d", tt.a, tt.b), func(t *testing.T) {

        result := Add(tt.a, tt.b)

        assert.Equal(t, tt.expected, result, "Expected result does not match")

    })

    }

}
```

In this example:

- **Test Cases**: A slice of test cases is defined, where each test case is a struct containing input values (a, b) and the expected result.
- **Looping Through Test Cases**: We loop through each test case using t.Run() to run subtests for each pair of inputs.
- **Assertions**: The result of calling Add(tt.a, tt.b) is compared to the expected value using assert.Equal().

3. Using Table-Driven Tests for Complex Logic

Table-driven tests are especially useful when dealing with more complex logic, like sorting algorithms or functions with multiple conditions. For example, you can use table-driven tests to validate that your sorting function correctly handles various edge cases like empty slices, already sorted slices, or slices with duplicate values.

In this section, we explored the testify package, which extends the functionality of Go's built-in testing package with more powerful assertions, mocks, and utilities for easier testing. The package simplifies writing unit tests and managing test expectations, which is especially helpful when working on large applications.

We also learned how to write table-driven tests, a pattern that allows you to efficiently test multiple input-output combinations with a single test function. This approach improves test maintainability, scalability, and readability.

By leveraging testify and table-driven tests, you'll be able to write more expressive and efficient tests, ensuring that your Go programs are robust and free from bugs.

Benchmarking Performance with go test -bench

Performance benchmarks are an essential part of ensuring your code runs efficiently. In Go, you can use the built-in testing package to write benchmarks. By running benchmarks, you can identify slow code paths, compare different implementation strategies, and track performance improvements over time.

---

1. Writing a Benchmark Function

A benchmark function in Go starts with Benchmark and takes a pointer to a testing.B struct. The b.N value represents the number of iterations the benchmark should run. Your benchmark code runs inside a loop that executes b.N times.

Example: Simple Benchmark

go

Copy

```
package main

import (
        "strings"
        "testing"
)


func ConcatenateWithPlusOperator(strs []string) string {
        result := ""
        for _, s := range strs {
                result += s
        }
}
```

```
    return result

}


func BenchmarkConcatenateWithPlusOperator(b *testing.B) {

    strs := []string{"Hello", " ", "world", "!", " Go", " ", "is", " ", "awesome", "!"}

    for i := 0; i < b.N; i++ {

        _ = ConcatenateWithPlusOperator(strs)

    }

}
```

Explanation:

- The benchmark function is named BenchmarkConcatenateWithPlusOperator.
- It repeatedly calls ConcatenateWithPlusOperator(strs) in a loop b.N times.
- The b.N value automatically adjusts to provide a stable performance measurement.

---

2. Running Benchmarks

Use go test -bench to run benchmarks. By default, go test runs both tests and benchmarks. To focus only on benchmarks, you can run:

bash

Copy

```
go test -bench=.
```

This will execute all benchmark functions in the current package and print performance results.

Sample Output:

bash

Copy

```
BenchmarkConcatenateWithPlusOperator-8      12345678    89.2 ns/op
```

- 12345678: The number of iterations run by the benchmark.
- 89.2 ns/op: The average time per operation (nanoseconds per loop iteration).

---

3. Comparing Implementations

Benchmarks help you compare different implementations of the same functionality. For example, you could benchmark using a strings.Builder instead of the + operator to concatenate strings.

Example: Benchmarking strings.Builder

go

Copy

```go
func ConcatenateWithBuilder(strs []string) string {

    var builder strings.Builder

    for _, s := range strs {

        builder.WriteString(s)

    }

    return builder.String()

}


func BenchmarkConcatenateWithBuilder(b *testing.B) {

    strs := []string{"Hello", " ", "world", "!", " Go", " ", "is", " ", "awesome", "!"}

    for i := 0; i < b.N; i++ {

        _ = ConcatenateWithBuilder(strs)

    }

}
```

You can run both benchmarks side by side and compare their results. If strings.Builder is faster, you might decide to use it in your code.

- **locals**: Show all local variables in the current scope.
- **goroutines**: List all active goroutines.
- **stack**: Show the current call stack.
- **restart**: Restart the program.
- **quit**: Exit the debugger.

---

4. Using Breakpoints

Breakpoints let you pause execution at specific points in your code to inspect the program state.

Example: Setting a Breakpoint at a Function

bash

Copy

```
break main.main
```

Example: Setting a Breakpoint at a Specific Line

bash

Copy

```
break main.go:15
```

Once the breakpoint is hit, you can use print to check variable values, stack to view the call stack, and next or step to move through the code.

5. Examining Goroutines and Concurrency Issues

Concurrency issues, like race conditions or deadlocks, are often hard to diagnose. Delve provides commands to inspect goroutines and their states.

- **goroutines**: List all goroutines. This helps identify if some goroutines are stuck or in unexpected states.
- **goroutine <id>**: Focus on a specific goroutine.
- **stack** (after focusing on a goroutine): Show the call stack for that goroutine.

By examining goroutine stacks, you can find out why a program is hanging or not performing as expected.

6. Exploring Variables and Memory

To inspect variables, use the print command. For example:

bash

Copy

```
print myVariable
```

This command prints the value of myVariable. You can also evaluate complex expressions or dereference pointers.

7. Debugging Tests with Delve

Delve can also debug Go tests. Simply run:

bash

Copy

dlv test

This command runs your test binary inside Delve, letting you step through test logic, inspect variables, and identify why tests are failing.

Benchmarking and debugging are critical tools for producing efficient, reliable Go applications. By using go test -bench, you can measure and optimize your code's performance, comparing different approaches and tracking improvements over time. Meanwhile, the Delve debugger empowers you to investigate issues, inspect program state, and step through code to find the root causes of bugs and unexpected behavior.

Together, these tools help ensure that your Go code runs as efficiently and correctly as possible.

Chapter 13: Deploying and Running Go Applications

One of Go's greatest strengths is its ability to produce small, standalone binaries that are easy to deploy. Once you've written and tested your code, deploying a Go application is straightforward. In this chapter, we'll explore how to compile Go programs for various platforms, understand the concept of cross-compilation, and learn best practices for deploying your Go applications.

Compiling Go Programs for Different Platforms

Go applications are typically compiled into a single binary file that can be directly executed on the target system. This approach eliminates dependencies and simplifies deployment—no additional runtime or libraries are required.

1. Basic Compilation

By default, running go build compiles your code for the platform you're currently on. For example, if you're on a Linux machine, running go build produces a binary that runs on Linux.

bash
Copy
```
go build -o myapp
```

This command generates a binary named myapp. You can then copy this binary to the target environment and run it.

Example on Linux:

bash

Copy

./myapp

Example on macOS:

bash

Copy

./myapp

Example on Windows:

bash

Copy

myapp.exe

---

2. Specifying Output Names and Paths

The -o flag allows you to specify the name and location of the output binary:

bash

Copy

go build -o /path/to/output/myapp

This is helpful when organizing build artifacts or when you want to produce a binary with a specific name.

3. Adding Build Tags

Build tags are a feature that lets you include or exclude certain files or code based on conditions. For example, you might have platform-specific code that only compiles on Linux or Windows.

Using Build Tags:

Add a comment at the top of your file:

go

Copy

```
// +build linux
```

Run the build command specifying the tag:

bash

Copy

```
go build -tags=linux
```

Understanding Cross-Compilation

Cross-compilation refers to building a binary on one platform that runs on another. Go makes this process incredibly simple. You can set environment variables to target different operating systems and architectures without requiring separate toolchains or complex configurations.

1. Using GOOS and GOARCH

Go uses two environment variables to control cross-compilation:

- **GOOS**: Specifies the target operating system (e.g., linux, darwin for macOS, windows).

343

- **GOARCH**: Specifies the target CPU architecture (e.g., amd64, 386, arm).

Example: Cross-Compiling for Linux on a macOS System:

bash

Copy

```
GOOS=linux GOARCH=amd64 go build -o myapp-linux
```

Example: Cross-Compiling for Windows:

bash

Copy

```
GOOS=windows GOARCH=amd64 go build -o myapp.exe
```

Example: Cross-Compiling for ARM (e.g., Raspberry Pi):

bash

Copy

```
GOOS=linux GOARCH=arm GOARM=7 go build -o myapp-arm
```

After running these commands, you'll have a binary that can be transferred and executed on the target platform.

---

2. Cross-Compiling Best Practices

- **Test on the Target Platform**: Even though the binary compiles, it's always a good idea to test it on the actual target platform to ensure everything behaves as expected.

- **Check External Dependencies**: If your application relies on system-specific libraries or tools, make sure they are available on the target environment. While Go's standard library is cross-platform, external dependencies might not be.
- **Minimize Platform-Specific Code**: Try to write code that works across platforms. Use build tags and platform checks only when absolutely necessary.

---

3. Distributing Binaries

Once you've compiled your application, distributing it is as simple as copying the binary to the target machine. If needed, you can compress the binary into a ZIP or tarball for easier transfer.

Common Steps:

1. Compile the binary for the target platform.

Compress it (if desired):
bash
Copy
```
tar -czvf myapp-linux-amd64.tar.gz myapp
```
or
bash
Copy
```
zip myapp-windows-amd64.zip myapp.exe
```
2. Transfer the binary to the target machine (e.g., using SCP, SFTP, or a file-sharing service).

Unpack (if compressed) and run it:
bash

```
tar -xzvf myapp-linux-amd64.tar.gz
./myapp
```

- **Single Binary Deployment**: One of Go's biggest advantages is the ability to compile programs into a single, self-contained binary. This simplifies the deployment process since you don't need to worry about installing dependencies on the target system.
- **Cross-Platform Builds**: With GOOS and GOARCH, you can easily produce binaries for multiple platforms from a single development machine. This makes Go a great choice for building tools and services that run on diverse environments.
- **Ease of Distribution**: Once compiled, Go binaries can be distributed and run directly. This makes deployment pipelines simpler, as you only need to copy and run the compiled binary.

By leveraging Go's powerful compilation model and straightforward cross-compilation process, you can focus on writing code rather than worrying about deployment complexity.

Deploying a Go Web App on AWS, DigitalOcean, or Heroku

When it comes to deploying a Go web application, there are many cloud providers and platforms to choose from. In this section, we'll cover the basics of deploying a Go web app on three popular options: AWS, DigitalOcean, and Heroku.

1. Deploying on AWS

AWS offers a wide range of services and deployment options for running Go applications. Two common approaches are using **Elastic Beanstalk** or setting up a virtual server with **EC2**.

Using Elastic Beanstalk:

- Elastic Beanstalk simplifies the deployment process by handling provisioning, scaling, and load balancing for your application.
- You can deploy a Go web app by:
    1. Creating a Go binary and a deployment package (e.g., a zip file containing the binary and a Procfile).
    2. Using the AWS Elastic Beanstalk CLI to create and deploy the environment.
    3. Letting Elastic Beanstalk manage the infrastructure and scale your application as traffic grows.

Using EC2:

- EC2 offers more control over your environment. You can:
    1. Launch a virtual server.
    2. Install your Go binary and its dependencies.
    3. Set up a reverse proxy (e.g., Nginx) to forward HTTP traffic to your Go app.
    4. Use systemd or another process manager to ensure your app runs as a service.

---

2. Deploying on DigitalOcean

DigitalOcean is known for its simplicity and ease of use, making it a popular choice for developers.

Using Droplets (Virtual Servers):

- Create a Droplet (DigitalOcean's name for a virtual server) with your desired operating system.
- SSH into the Droplet and:
    1. Upload your Go binary.
    2. Set up a web server or reverse proxy if needed (Nginx or Caddy are common choices).
    3. Configure a firewall and TLS certificates (e.g., with Let's Encrypt) to secure your application.
    4. Run your application using a process manager like systemd to keep it running and restart it if it crashes.

Using DigitalOcean App Platform:

- The App Platform is a fully managed platform-as-a-service (PaaS).
- You can push your code to GitHub and connect it to the App Platform.
- DigitalOcean handles the deployment, scaling, and infrastructure for you.

---

3. Deploying on Heroku

Heroku is a PaaS that focuses on ease of deployment and developer productivity. It's a great option if you want to avoid managing servers directly.

Steps to Deploy a Go App on Heroku:

1. **Prepare Your Codebase**:

Make sure you have a Procfile to tell Heroku how to run your application. For a Go web app, it might look like:

bash

Copy

```
web: ./myapp
```

- Add a go.mod file to define your dependencies.

Install the Heroku CLI:

bash

Copy

```
curl https://cli-assets.heroku.com/install.sh | sh
```

2. **Create a Heroku App**:

   bash

   Copy

   ```
   heroku create
   ```

3. **Push Your Code**:
   - Initialize a Git repository (if you haven't already).

Commit your code and push it to Heroku:

bash

Copy

```
git push heroku main
```

4. **Scale and Monitor**:

Scale your application by increasing the number of dynos:

bash

Copy

```
heroku ps:scale web=1
```

      ○

Monitor logs and performance:

bash

Copy

```
heroku logs --tail
```

Using Docker to Containerize Go Applications

Containerization is a popular approach to building, deploying, and running applications consistently across multiple environments. Docker simplifies the process by packaging your application and all its dependencies into a lightweight container image.

---

1. What is Docker?

Docker is a platform that enables you to:

- Create portable container images.
- Run containers on any system with Docker installed.
- Simplify application deployment by standardizing the environment.

---

2. Writing a Dockerfile for Your Go App

A **Dockerfile** is a set of instructions to build a Docker image. For a Go web app, a typical Dockerfile might look like this:

dockerfile

Copy

```
# Step 1: Use the official Go image to compile the application

FROM golang:1.19 AS build


# Set the working directory inside the container

WORKDIR /app


# Copy the go.mod and go.sum files to cache dependencies

COPY go.mod go.sum ./


# Download dependencies

RUN go mod download


# Copy the source code into the container

COPY . .
```

```
# Build the Go application

RUN go build -o myapp


# Step 2: Use a minimal image to run the application

FROM alpine:latest


# Set the working directory

WORKDIR /root/


# Copy the binary from the builder stage

COPY --from=build /app/myapp .


# Expose the port the app runs on

EXPOSE 8080


# Command to run the application

CMD ["./myapp"]
```

3. Building and Running the Docker Image

Build the Image:

bash

Copy

```
docker build -t myapp:latest .
```

Run the Container:

bash

Copy

```
docker run -p 8080:8080 myapp:latest
```

This command maps port 8080 on your local machine to port 8080 inside the container, allowing you to access your Go web app at http://localhost:8080.

---

4. Benefits of Using Docker

- **Consistent Environments**: Containers ensure your application runs the same way in development, testing, and production.
- **Simplified Dependencies**: All dependencies are bundled inside the container, eliminating issues related to missing libraries or versions.

- **Easy Scaling**: Docker works well with container orchestration platforms like Kubernetes, making it easier to scale applications horizontally.

CI/CD Pipelines for Go Applications

Continuous Integration (CI) and Continuous Deployment (CD) pipelines automate the process of building, testing, and deploying your Go applications. This ensures that new changes are thoroughly tested before they reach production and that deployments are quick, reliable, and repeatable.

---

1. Setting Up CI with GitHub Actions

GitHub Actions is a popular CI/CD platform integrated into GitHub. It's free for open-source projects and easy to set up.

Example Workflow:

yaml

Copy

```
# .github/workflows/go.yml

name: Go CI


on:

  push:
```

```yaml
    branches:

      - main

  pull_request:

    branches:

      - main


jobs:

  build:

    runs-on: ubuntu-latest


    steps:

      - name: Checkout code

        uses: actions/checkout@v3


      - name: Set up Go

        uses: actions/setup-go@v3

        with:

          go-version: 1.19
```

```
- name: Install dependencies

  run: go mod tidy


- name: Run tests

  run: go test ./...


- name: Build binary

  run: go build -o myapp
```

This workflow:

1. Triggers on pushes or pull requests to the main branch.
2. Sets up a Go environment, installs dependencies, runs tests, and builds the application.

---

2. Adding CD to the Pipeline

You can extend this workflow to deploy your application automatically. For example, after a successful build, you might:

- Push a Docker image to a container registry (like Docker Hub or Amazon ECR).
- Deploy the container to a Kubernetes cluster or a cloud provider.

---

3. Benefits of CI/CD Pipelines

- **Faster Feedback Loops**: Developers get immediate feedback if their changes break the build or cause test failures.
- **Increased Reliability**: By automating tests and deployments, you reduce human error.
- **Easier Collaboration**: Teams can confidently merge changes knowing that the CI pipeline ensures quality.

Deploying and running Go applications becomes straightforward when you leverage platforms like AWS, DigitalOcean, or Heroku. Containerizing with Docker ensures consistency and simplifies deployment, while CI/CD pipelines streamline the process of building, testing, and releasing your code. Together, these approaches make it easy to develop, deliver, and scale Go applications efficiently.

Chapter 14: Final Project: Building a Complete Web Service

In this final chapter, we'll walk through the process of building a fully functioning web service from start to finish. The project will be a simple user management system that includes user authentication and basic CRUD operations for managing profiles. Along the way, you'll learn how to structure your code, implement secure authentication, and lay the groundwork for a scalable web application.

Setting Up the Project Structure

A well-organized project structure helps keep your codebase maintainable as it grows. While there's no single "correct" way to structure a Go project, it's common to separate concerns into logical packages and directories.

1. Common Directories in a Go Web Project

cmd/: Contains the entry point for your application.

Example:

plaintext

Copy

```
cmd/
└── user-service/
    └── main.go
```

- internal/: Holds application-specific code that should not be exposed as a public API.

  Example:

plaintext

Copy

internal/

```
├── auth/
│   ├── auth.go
│   └── middleware.go
├── user/
│   ├── user.go
│   └── user_service.go
└── db/
    └── database.go
```

- **pkg/**: (Optional) Contains reusable code that might be shared across different projects.

api/: Stores API-specific code, like request handlers, response types, and routing configuration.

Example:

plaintext

Copy

api/

```
├── handlers/
│   ├── user_handler.go
│   └── auth_handler.go
└── routes.go
```

- **configs/**: Holds configuration files (YAML, JSON, or TOML) that define environment-specific settings.

2. Example Project Layout

plaintext

Copy

```
user-service/
├── cmd/
│   └── user-service/
│       └── main.go
├── internal/
│   ├── auth/
│   │   ├── auth.go
│   │   └── middleware.go
│   ├── user/
│   │   ├── user.go
│   │   └── user_service.go
│   └── db/
│       └── database.go
├── api/
│   ├── handlers/
│   │   ├── user_handler.go
│   │   └── auth_handler.go
│   └── routes.go
├── configs/
│   └── config.yaml
└── go.mod
```

Creating a User Authentication System

Authentication is a critical part of any web service that handles user accounts. In this section, we'll create a simple, secure user authentication system that uses hashed passwords and JSON Web Tokens (JWTs) for user sessions.

1. Setting Up the User Model

First, define a basic user model. This will be used to store user information in your database.

internal/user/user.go:

go
Copy

```go
package user

import "time"

// User represents a user in the system
type User struct {
    ID        int       `json:"id"`
    Username  string    `json:"username"`
    Password  string    `json:"-"`
    CreatedAt time.Time `json:"created_at"`
    UpdatedAt time.Time `json:"updated_at"`
}
```

Explanation:

- The Password field is not included in JSON responses to ensure it is never exposed in API outputs.
- The CreatedAt and UpdatedAt fields help keep track of when the user was added or modified.

---

2. Handling Password Hashing

Instead of storing plain-text passwords, you'll hash them before saving them to the database. When a user attempts to log in, you'll hash the provided password and compare it to the stored hash.

internal/auth/auth.go:

go
Copy

```go
package auth

import (
    "golang.org/x/crypto/bcrypt"
)

// HashPassword hashes a plaintext password
func HashPassword(password string) (string, error) {
    hashedBytes, err := bcrypt.GenerateFromPassword([]byte(password),
bcrypt.DefaultCost)
    return string(hashedBytes), err
}
```

```
// ComparePassword compares a plaintext password with a hashed password
func ComparePassword(hashedPassword, password string) error {
    return bcrypt.CompareHashAndPassword([]byte(hashedPassword), []byte(password))
}
```

Explanation:

- HashPassword: Uses bcrypt to hash a password before saving it to the database.
- ComparePassword: Compares a provided password with a stored hash during login. If the passwords don't match, it returns an error.

---

3. Generating JWTs

Once a user logs in successfully, you'll issue a JSON Web Token (JWT) that the client can use to authenticate future requests. The token includes user data and is signed with a secret key.

internal/auth/jwt.go:

go
Copy
```
package auth

import (
    "time"
    "github.com/golang-jwt/jwt/v4"
)

// Claims defines the structure of the JWT claims
```

```go
type Claims struct {
    UserID int `json:"user_id"`
    jwt.RegisteredClaims
}

// GenerateToken creates a JWT for the given user ID
func GenerateToken(userID int, secretKey string) (string, error) {
    claims := Claims{
        UserID: userID,
        RegisteredClaims: jwt.RegisteredClaims{
            ExpiresAt: jwt.NewNumericDate(time.Now().Add(24 * time.Hour)),
            IssuedAt:  jwt.NewNumericDate(time.Now()),
        },
    }

    token := jwt.NewWithClaims(jwt.SigningMethodHS256, claims)
    return token.SignedString([]byte(secretKey))
}

// ValidateToken parses and validates a JWT
func ValidateToken(tokenStr, secretKey string) (*Claims, error) {
    token, err := jwt.ParseWithClaims(tokenStr, &Claims{}, func(token *jwt.Token)
(interface{}, error) {
        return []byte(secretKey), nil
    })

    if err != nil {
        return nil, err
    }
```

```go
    claims, ok := token.Claims.(*Claims)
    if !ok || !token.Valid {
        return nil, jwt.ErrSignatureInvalid
    }

    return claims, nil
}
```

Explanation:

- **GenerateToken**: Creates a JWT that contains the user's ID and expiration time.
- **ValidateToken**: Parses the JWT to ensure it is valid and was signed with the correct secret key.

---

4. Setting Up Authentication Routes

You can now create API routes to register users and log them in. These routes will hash passwords, store user information, and return JWTs.

api/handlers/auth_handler.go:

go
Copy
```go
package handlers

import (
    "encoding/json"
    "net/http"
```

```
    "internal/auth"
    "internal/user"
)

var secretKey = "mySecretKey" // This should be stored securely (e.g., in environment
variables)

// RegisterUser handles user registration
func RegisterUser(w http.ResponseWriter, r *http.Request) {
    var newUser user.User
    if err := json.NewDecoder(r.Body).Decode(&newUser); err != nil {
        http.Error(w, "Invalid input", http.StatusBadRequest)
        return
    }

    hashedPassword, err := auth.HashPassword(newUser.Password)
    if err != nil {
        http.Error(w, "Failed to hash password", http.StatusInternalServerError)
        return
    }
    newUser.Password = hashedPassword

    // Save the newUser to your database here (omitted for brevity)

    w.WriteHeader(http.StatusCreated)
    json.NewEncoder(w).Encode(newUser)
}

// LoginUser handles user login
```

```go
func LoginUser(w http.ResponseWriter, r *http.Request) {
    var loginUser user.User
    if err := json.NewDecoder(r.Body).Decode(&loginUser); err != nil {
        http.Error(w, "Invalid input", http.StatusBadRequest)
        return
    }

    // Fetch user from database here (omitted for brevity)

    // Check the password
    if err := auth.ComparePassword("stored_hashed_password", loginUser.Password); err != nil {
        http.Error(w, "Invalid credentials", http.StatusUnauthorized)
        return
    }

    // Generate JWT
    token, err := auth.GenerateToken(loginUser.ID, secretKey)
    if err != nil {
        http.Error(w, "Failed to generate token", http.StatusInternalServerError)
        return
    }

    json.NewEncoder(w).Encode(map[string]string{"token": token})
}
```

At this stage, you've set up a foundational project structure and implemented a basic user authentication system. This system includes hashed passwords for security, JWTs for user sessions, and clearly defined APIs for registering and logging in users.

Next, you'll expand the web service by adding more features, improving database integration, and building out the full CRUD operations.

Implementing JWT-Based Authentication

With JWTs (JSON Web Tokens), you can securely manage user sessions without relying on traditional server-side sessions or cookies. Let's break down how to fully implement JWT-based authentication in your Go web service.

---

1. Generating Tokens Upon Login

When a user successfully logs in, you'll issue a JWT. The token includes the user's ID and an expiration time, and it's signed with a secret key. This token is then returned to the client, which stores it (typically in localStorage, sessionStorage, or a cookie) and includes it in the Authorization header of future requests.

Example: Issuing a JWT

go
Copy
```
package auth

import (
        "time"
        "github.com/golang-jwt/jwt/v4"
)
```

```go
type Claims struct {
        UserID int `json:"user_id"`
        jwt.RegisteredClaims
}

func GenerateToken(userID int, secretKey string) (string, error) {
        claims := Claims{
                UserID: userID,
                RegisteredClaims: jwt.RegisteredClaims{
                        ExpiresAt: jwt.NewNumericDate(time.Now().Add(24 *
time.Hour)),
                        IssuedAt:  jwt.NewNumericDate(time.Now()),
                },
        }
        token := jwt.NewWithClaims(jwt.SigningMethodHS256, claims)
        return token.SignedString([]byte(secretKey))
}
```

- **UserID**: The payload typically contains user-related information (like a unique identifier) so that the server can later recognize which user sent the request.
- **Expiration Time**: The ExpiresAt claim sets when the token will expire.

---

2. Validating Tokens on Requests

To protect certain endpoints (like /profile or /dashboard), you need middleware that checks for a valid JWT in the incoming request's headers.

Example: JWT Middleware

go

Copy

```go
package auth

import (
        "context"
        "net/http"
)

type contextKey string

const UserIDKey contextKey = "userID"

func JWTMiddleware(secretKey string, next http.Handler) http.Handler {
        return http.HandlerFunc(func(w http.ResponseWriter, r *http.Request) {
                authHeader := r.Header.Get("Authorization")
                if authHeader == "" {
                        http.Error(w, "Authorization header missing",
http.StatusUnauthorized)
                        return
                }

                // Parse the token
                tokenStr := authHeader[len("Bearer "):]
                claims, err := ValidateToken(tokenStr, secretKey)
                if err != nil {
                        http.Error(w, "Invalid token", http.StatusUnauthorized)
                        return
```

```
        }

        // Add the user ID to the request context
        ctx := context.WithValue(r.Context(), UserIDKey, claims.UserID)
        next.ServeHTTP(w, r.WithContext(ctx))
    })
}

func ValidateToken(tokenStr, secretKey string) (*Claims, error) {
    token, err := jwt.ParseWithClaims(tokenStr, &Claims{}, func(token *jwt.Token)
(interface{}, error) {
        return []byte(secretKey), nil
    })
    if err != nil || !token.Valid {
        return nil, err
    }
    return token.Claims.(*Claims), nil
}
```

- **JWTMiddleware**: Checks for the Authorization header, validates the JWT, and, if valid, extracts the user ID and stores it in the request context.
- **Context Key**: Using a context key lets downstream handlers retrieve the user ID from the request context.

---

3. Using JWT Middleware

To protect an endpoint, wrap it with the middleware:

Example: Protected Endpoint

go

Copy

```go
package handlers

import (
        "encoding/json"
        "net/http"
        "internal/auth"
)

func ProtectedEndpoint(w http.ResponseWriter, r *http.Request) {
        userID := r.Context().Value(auth.UserIDKey)
        if userID == nil {
                http.Error(w, "Unauthorized", http.StatusUnauthorized)
                return
        }
        json.NewEncoder(w).Encode(map[string]interface{}{
                "userID": userID,
                "message": "Welcome to the protected endpoint!",
        })
}
```

By using auth.JWTMiddleware(secretKey, handler), you can ensure that only requests with valid tokens reach this handler.

Connecting to a Database with GORM

GORM is a popular Go ORM (Object-Relational Mapper) that simplifies working with databases. It provides an abstraction layer for common database operations, making it easier to manage records and relationships without writing raw SQL.

---

1. Setting Up GORM

To start using GORM, first install it:

bash
Copy

```
go get -u gorm.io/gorm
go get -u gorm.io/driver/sqlite
```

You can use other drivers (like PostgreSQL or MySQL), but for simplicity, let's use SQLite in this example.

---

2. Initializing a GORM Connection

Example: Connecting to SQLite

go
Copy

```
package db

import (
        "gorm.io/driver/sqlite"
```

```go
        "gorm.io/gorm"
)

func ConnectDatabase() (*gorm.DB, error) {
        db, err := gorm.Open(sqlite.Open("test.db"), &gorm.Config{})
        if err != nil {
                return nil, err
        }
        return db, nil
}
```

For production environments, you might use PostgreSQL:

bash

Copy

```bash
go get -u gorm.io/driver/postgres
```

Example: PostgreSQL Connection

go

Copy

```go
package db

import (
        "gorm.io/driver/postgres"
        "gorm.io/gorm"
)

func ConnectDatabase() (*gorm.DB, error) {
```

```go
        dsn := "host=localhost user=postgres password=secret dbname=mydb port=5432
sslmode=disable"
        db, err := gorm.Open(postgres.Open(dsn), &gorm.Config{})
        if err != nil {
                return nil, err
        }
        return db, nil
}
```

---

3. Defining Models

GORM uses structs to define database models. For instance, you might have a User struct that maps to a users table.

Example: Defining a User Model

```go
go
Copy
package user

import "gorm.io/gorm"

type User struct {
        gorm.Model
        Username string `gorm:"uniqueIndex"`
        Password string
}
```

- **gorm.Model**: Includes common fields like ID, CreatedAt, UpdatedAt, and DeletedAt.
- **uniqueIndex**: Ensures that the Username field must be unique in the database.

---

4. Auto-Migrating Models

GORM can automatically create or update tables to match your model definitions:

Example: Auto-Migrate

go
Copy
```
package db

import (
        "gorm.io/gorm"
        "user-service/internal/user"
)

func AutoMigrate(db *gorm.DB) error {
        return db.AutoMigrate(&user.User{})
}
```

When you call AutoMigrate, GORM ensures that the users table exists and matches the structure of the User model.

---

5. Performing CRUD Operations

GORM provides methods for all common CRUD (Create, Read, Update, Delete) operations.

Create a User:

go

Copy

```
newUser := user.User{Username: "testuser", Password: "hashedpassword"}
if err := db.Create(&newUser).Error; err != nil {
    // Handle error
}
```

- **Find a User:**

  go

  Copy

  ```
  var user user.User
  ```

```
if err := db.First(&user, "username = ?", "testuser").Error; err != nil {
    // Handle error (e.g., user not found)
}
```

- **Update a User:**

  go

  Copy

  ```
  user.Password = "newhashedpassword"
  ```

```
if err := db.Save(&user).Error; err != nil {
    // Handle error
}
```

377

- **Delete a User:**

go

Copy

```go
if err := db.Delete(&user).Error; err != nil {

    // Handle error

}
```

---

6. Integrating GORM and Authentication

When a user registers or logs in, you'll interact with the database to store or retrieve user records.

Example: Storing a Hashed Password

go

Copy

```go
hashedPassword, _ := auth.HashPassword("plaintextpassword")
newUser := user.User{Username: "testuser", Password: hashedPassword}
db.Create(&newUser)
```

Example: Validating a User During Login

go

Copy

```go
var foundUser user.User
if err := db.First(&foundUser, "username = ?", "testuser").Error; err != nil {
    // User not found
}
```

```
if err := auth.ComparePassword(foundUser.Password, "plaintextpassword"); err != nil {
    // Invalid password
}
```

Once validated, generate a JWT using the user's ID and return it to the client.

By combining JWT-based authentication with GORM for database operations, you can build a robust and secure user authentication system. GORM simplifies database interactions, while JWT provides a lightweight and scalable way to handle user sessions. Together, they form the foundation of a complete web service.

Adding Logging and Monitoring

Logging and monitoring are critical components of any production-grade web service. They help you understand what's happening in your application, diagnose issues, and ensure smooth operation over time.

---

1. Adding Structured Logging

While basic fmt.Println() statements might be fine during development, structured logging provides consistent, machine-readable logs that can be easily parsed and analyzed.

Using a Structured Logging Library:

- Popular libraries: **logrus, zap, zerolog**.
- Structured logs typically output JSON or another format that's easy for log aggregators to process.

Example: Using zap

go

Copy

```go
package logger

import (
    "go.uber.org/zap"
)

var log *zap.Logger

func InitLogger() error {
    var err error
    log, err = zap.NewProduction()
    if err != nil {
        return err
    }
    defer log.Sync() // flushes buffer, if any
    return nil
```

```go
}


func GetLogger() *zap.Logger {

        return log

}
```

In your main code, you would initialize the logger and use it consistently:

go

Copy

```go
import "myapp/logger"


func main() {

        err := logger.InitLogger()

        if err != nil {

                panic("failed to initialize logger")

        }


        logger.GetLogger().Info("Application started", zap.String("version", "1.0.0"))

}
```

2. Implementing Contextual Logging

When handling requests, adding context to logs can help trace individual requests through the system. For example, you might include:

- **Request IDs**: Generated per request and logged to trace a user's activity.
- **User IDs**: If available, add them to logs to diagnose user-specific issues.
- **Timestamps**: Although most libraries add these by default, ensure you keep them consistent.

Using Request IDs in Logs:

go

Copy

```go
func requestLogger(next http.Handler) http.Handler {

    return http.HandlerFunc(func(w http.ResponseWriter, r *http.Request) {

        requestID := r.Header.Get("X-Request-ID")

        if requestID == "" {

            requestID = generateNewRequestID() // Implement a function to generate unique IDs

        }

        logger.GetLogger().Info("Incoming request",
```

```
            zap.String("requestID", requestID),

            zap.String("method", r.Method),

            zap.String("url", r.URL.Path),

        )

        next.ServeHTTP(w, r)

    })

}
```

---

3. Adding Monitoring

Beyond logging, monitoring tracks key metrics to provide insights into your application's health and performance. Common monitoring tools include **Prometheus**, **Grafana**, and **New Relic**.

Expose Metrics Using Prometheus:

- Import a Prometheus client library (e.g., github.com/prometheus/client_golang).
- Create and register metrics such as request counters, latency histograms, and error rates.
- Serve metrics at a dedicated endpoint (e.g., /metrics) so a Prometheus server can scrape them.

Example: Basic Prometheus Metric

go

Copy

```go
package metrics

import (

        "github.com/prometheus/client_golang/prometheus"

        "github.com/prometheus/client_golang/prometheus/promhttp"

        "net/http"

)

var (

        httpRequests = prometheus.NewCounterVec(

                prometheus.CounterOpts{

                        Name: "http_requests_total",

                        Help: "Total HTTP requests processed, categorized by status code
and method.",

                },

                []string{"code", "method"},

        )

)
```

```go
func InitMetrics() {

    prometheus.MustRegister(httpRequests)

    http.Handle("/metrics", promhttp.Handler())

}


func RecordRequest(method, code string) {

    httpRequests.WithLabelValues(code, method).Inc()

}
```

Integrate Metrics Into Your Code:

go

Copy

```go
metrics.RecordRequest(r.Method, "200")
```

With this in place, Prometheus can scrape metrics and you can visualize them using a dashboard tool like Grafana.

Deploying the Web Service to a Cloud Server

Once your web service is ready, the next step is to deploy it to a production environment. Deploying to the cloud is a common choice, as it provides scalability, redundancy, and managed services.

---

1. Choosing a Cloud Provider

Popular options include:

- **AWS**: Offers a wide array of services, including EC2 (virtual servers), Elastic Beanstalk (PaaS), and Lambda (serverless).
- **Google Cloud Platform (GCP)**: Provides Compute Engine (VMs), App Engine (PaaS), and Kubernetes Engine.
- **Azure**: Includes Virtual Machines, App Services, and Kubernetes Service.
- **DigitalOcean**: Known for simplicity and affordable virtual servers (Droplets).
- **Heroku**: A developer-friendly platform-as-a-service that abstracts server management.

---

2. Preparing the Application for Deployment

Build a Release Binary:

- Use go build or go install to produce a production-ready binary.
- Consider statically compiling the binary if you need to run it on minimal container images.

Set Up Environment Variables:

- Store sensitive information (like database credentials, JWT secrets) in environment variables or use a secret management tool.
- Ensure your code reads configurations from environment variables, making it easier to change settings without modifying code.

---

3. Deploying to a Virtual Machine

Example: Deploying on AWS EC2 or a DigitalOcean Droplet

1. Spin up a virtual machine (e.g., AWS EC2 instance, DigitalOcean Droplet).

SSH into the server:

bash

Copy

```
ssh user@your-server-ip
```

2. Transfer your binary and configuration files:

   bash

   Copy

   ```
   scp myapp user@your-server-ip:/home/user/
   ```

3. Set up environment variables on the server:

   bash

   Copy

   ```
   export JWT_SECRET=mysecret
   ```

```
export DB_CONN_STRING="user:password@tcp(127.0.0.1:3306)/mydb"
```

4. Run your application:

bash

Copy

./myapp

5. (Optional) Use a process manager (like systemd) to run the application as a service:

Create a myapp.service file in /etc/systemd/system/ and include:

plaintext

Copy

[Unit]

Description=My Go Web Service

After=network.target

[Service]

ExecStart=/home/user/myapp

Restart=always

Environment=JWT_SECRET=mysecret

Environment=DB_CONN_STRING=user:password@tcp(127.0.0.1:3306)/mydb

[Install]

WantedBy=multi-user.target

- Enable and start the service:

bash

Copy

```
sudo systemctl enable myapp

sudo systemctl start myapp
```

-

---

4. Deploying Using Docker

Containerizing your application with Docker ensures consistency across environments and makes scaling easier.

Example: Dockerizing Your Go App

Create a Dockerfile:

dockerfile

Copy

```
FROM golang:1.19 AS build

WORKDIR /app

COPY go.mod go.sum ./

RUN go mod download

COPY . .

RUN go build -o myapp
```

```
FROM alpine:latest

WORKDIR /root/

COPY --from=build /app/myapp .

EXPOSE 8080

CMD ["./myapp"]
```

1. Build the image:
   bash

   Copy
   ```
   docker build -t myapp:latest .
   ```

2. Run the container:
   bash

   Copy
   ```
   docker run -p 8080:8080 myapp:latest
   ```

Deploying to Cloud Providers:

- Use container orchestration platforms like Kubernetes.
- Leverage cloud container services (AWS ECS, GCP Cloud Run, Azure Container Instances) to handle scaling and deployment.

---

5. Using Managed Services

For platforms like Heroku, you can:

- Push your code to a Git repository.
- Let the platform handle building, running, and scaling your app.

- Set environment variables via a simple command or web interface.
- Scale your application by increasing the number of dynos or instances.

Example: Deploying to Heroku

bash

Copy

```
git init

heroku create

git add .

git commit -m "Initial commit"

git push heroku main
```

Adding structured logging and monitoring ensures you can maintain and troubleshoot your web service once it's live. Deploying to a cloud server—whether via a virtual machine, Docker container, or a managed PaaS—gives you flexibility and scalability. With the right setup, you'll have a robust, observable application running in a production environment, ready to handle real-world traffic.

Chapter 15: Where to Go Next?

Congratulations on completing this guide! By now, you have a solid understanding of Go's fundamentals, how to build web services, and how to deploy them. The natural question now is: **What comes next?**

In this chapter, we'll explore advanced Go topics you might consider diving into, as well as recommended books, courses, and communities that can help you continue your Go journey.

Advanced Go Topics to Explore Next

Go is a versatile language with a broad ecosystem. Once you've mastered the basics, these advanced topics can deepen your understanding and expand your capabilities:

1. Concurrency and Parallelism

- **Advanced Channel Patterns**:
  Go's concurrency model revolves around goroutines and channels. Exploring patterns like fan-out/fan-in, worker pools, and pipeline patterns can help you handle complex concurrency scenarios more effectively.
- **sync and atomic Packages**:
  For low-level concurrency control, Go offers primitives in the sync and sync/atomic packages. Learning these can help you fine-tune performance and handle shared state safely.

2. Memory Management and Profiling

- **Memory Profiling**:
  Use Go's built-in profiling tools (via pprof) to understand memory usage, identify leaks, and optimize allocation patterns.

- **Garbage Collection**:
  Although Go's garbage collector is automatic, understanding how it works can help you write more efficient code. Dive into how garbage collection affects latency and throughput in high-performance applications.

3. Error Handling and Debugging

- **Custom Error Types**:
  Go's error handling model is explicit, but you can go beyond errors.New() by creating custom error types, using fmt.Errorf with formatting, and introducing error wrapping for richer context.

- **Testing Beyond Unit Tests**:
  Move on to integration tests, property-based testing, and fuzz testing. Tools like go test -fuzz help you discover edge cases and improve code robustness.

4. Advanced Networking and APIs

- **gRPC and Protocol Buffers**:
  If you've been building REST APIs, gRPC is a natural next step. It's a high-performance framework that uses Protocol Buffers (protobufs) for efficient data serialization.

- **WebSocket Communication**:
  Explore real-time communication by integrating WebSockets into your applications. This is especially useful for building chat apps, live dashboards, and collaborative tools.

5. Advanced Build and Deployment Strategies

- **Multi-Stage Docker Builds**:
  Learn how to create leaner, more secure container images by using multi-stage builds.
- **Cross-Platform Releases**:
  Go's cross-compilation capabilities let you ship binaries for multiple platforms. Investigate how to streamline the release process for diverse operating systems and architectures.

6. Distributed Systems and Microservices

- **Service Discovery and Load Balancing**:
  Tools like Consul, Etcd, and gRPC's built-in service discovery features allow you to manage a network of services.
- **Distributed Tracing**:
  Integrate distributed tracing tools (e.g., OpenTelemetry) to monitor and optimize interactions between microservices.

Recommended Books, Courses, and Communities

There's a wealth of resources out there to keep learning and improving. Below are some standout options.

Books

- **"The Go Programming Language" by Alan A. A. Donovan and Brian W. Kernighan**:
  A comprehensive introduction to Go, covering both basics and advanced topics, written by some of the language's most respected contributors.

- **"Concurrency in Go" by Katherine Cox-Buday**:
  An in-depth exploration of Go's concurrency model, offering practical patterns and strategies for writing concurrent programs.
- **"Go in Action" by William Kennedy, Brian Ketelsen, and Erik St. Martin**:
  A hands-on guide that provides real-world examples and best practices for building production-ready Go applications.
- **"Practical Go" by Alex Edwards**:
  Focused on idiomatic Go and best practices, this book helps you understand how to write maintainable and efficient Go code.

Online Courses

- **"Justforfunc: Programming in Go" (YouTube series by Francesc Campoy)**:
  A free, high-quality series of videos on practical Go topics, ranging from the standard library to advanced patterns.
- **"Gophercises" by Jon Calhoun**:
  A collection of coding exercises and mini-projects designed to deepen your Go skills.
- **Udemy and Pluralsight Go Courses**:
  Both platforms offer beginner-to-advanced courses on Go. Look for instructors like Todd McLeod or Nigel Poulton for well-structured content.

Online Communities

- **Go Forum (forum.golangbridge.org)**:
  A welcoming space for Go developers of all levels. You can ask questions, share ideas, and learn from the community's collective experience.
- **Gopher Slack (invite.slack.golangbridge.org)**:
  A vibrant Slack community with channels dedicated to everything from general Go questions to specific topics like tools, libraries, and concurrency.

- **Reddit's r/golang**:
  A popular subreddit where you can stay up-to-date with the latest Go news, libraries, and discussion threads.
- **GopherCon and Local Meetups**:
  Consider attending Go conferences and meetups. GopherCon is the flagship conference, offering keynotes, workshops, and networking opportunities.

You've reached the end of this guide, but your Go journey is just beginning. By exploring advanced topics, tapping into high-quality resources, and engaging with the community, you can continue building your expertise and tackling increasingly complex projects. The Go ecosystem is rich with possibilities—whether you want to dive deeper into concurrency, optimize performance, or expand into distributed systems, there's always something new to learn.

Appendices

Appendix A: Useful Go Commands and Shortcuts

A solid understanding of Go's tools and commands can significantly boost your productivity. Here's a quick reference guide to commonly used Go commands and useful shortcuts:

1. Build and Run Commands

go build:

Compiles the code and produces a binary in the current directory.

bash

Copy

go build

- **go run:**

  Compiles and immediately runs the code without generating a binary.

  bash

  Copy

  go run main.go

- **go install:**

  Compiles and installs the binary in your $GOPATH/bin or $GOBIN directory.

  bash

  Copy

  go install

2. Testing and Benchmarking

go test:

Runs tests in the current package.

bash

Copy

go test ./...

- **go test -v**:

  Runs tests and prints detailed output.

  bash

  Copy

  go test -v

- **go test -bench .**:

  Runs benchmarks.

  bash

  Copy

  go test -bench=.

3. Code Management

go mod init:

Initializes a new Go module.

bash

Copy

go mod init mymodule

- **go mod tidy**:

  Cleans up unused dependencies.

  bash

  Copy

  go mod tidy

- go get:

  Adds or updates a dependency.

  bash

  Copy

  go get github.com/example/repo

4. Code Quality and Formatting

- go fmt ./...:

  Formats all Go files in the current module.

- go vet ./...:

  Analyzes code for potential errors.

- golangci-lint run:

  Runs a suite of linters (requires the golangci-lint tool).

Appendix B: Common Go Errors and How to Fix Them

1. cannot find package

- **Cause**:

  The module or package is not properly fetched or the import path is incorrect.

- **Fix**:

  Make sure go mod tidy has been run to download all dependencies.

  Double-check the import path and ensure it matches the module name.

2. undefined: <identifier>

- **Cause**:

  The code references a variable, function, or type that hasn't been declared or is not in scope.

- **Fix**:

  Check that the identifier is defined and correctly imported. If it's in another package, ensure you're using the correct package name.

3. import cycle not allowed

- **Cause**:

  Two or more packages import each other, creating a circular dependency.
- **Fix**:

  Refactor the code to break the cycle. Move shared code to a separate, common package that both can import.

4. nil pointer dereference

- **Cause**:

  A pointer is being used before it's initialized.
- **Fix**:

  Ensure pointers are properly initialized before use. Check for nil values before dereferencing.

5. too many open files

- **Cause**:

  The code opens files, connections, or resources without closing them, exhausting the system's limit.
- **Fix**:

  Close all opened files and connections. Use defer file.Close() right after opening a file to ensure it gets closed when no longer needed.

6. go mod tidy or go get hangs

- **Cause**:

  A dependency server is slow or unavailable.

- **Fix**:

  Check your internet connection, and if the issue persists, consider using a proxy like GOPROXY=proxy.golang.org.

Appendix C: Best Go Practices for Performance and Security

1. Performance Best Practices

- **Use Goroutines Wisely**:

  Concurrency can improve throughput, but too many goroutines can cause excessive memory usage or contention. Use sync.Pool or bounded worker pools to control concurrency levels.

- **Efficient Memory Allocation**:

  Minimize unnecessary memory allocations by reusing buffers and slices. Tools like go tool pprof can help identify memory hotspots.

- **Optimize I/O Operations**:

  Buffer I/O operations (using bufio) to reduce system calls. When processing large data sets, read and write in chunks instead of one line at a time.

- **Avoid Premature Optimization**:

  Write clear, idiomatic code first. Use profiling tools to identify actual bottlenecks before making optimizations.

2. Security Best Practices

- **Input Validation**:

  Always validate and sanitize user input, especially if it's used in database queries or passed to external services.

- **Use the crypto Package**:

  For cryptographic operations, rely on Go's standard crypto package rather than rolling your own.

- **Protect Secrets**:

  Don't hardcode sensitive information (e.g., API keys, database passwords). Store them in environment variables, secret management tools, or encrypted configuration files.

- **Keep Dependencies Updated**:

  Regularly run go mod tidy and go get -u to fetch the latest versions of your dependencies. Pay attention to security advisories for libraries you use.

- **Use Context for Timeouts and Deadlines**:

  Ensure requests have appropriate timeouts to prevent resource exhaustion. The context package is invaluable for handling timeouts and cancellation signals.

- **Static Analysis and Linters**:

  Use tools like golangci-lint and gosec to automatically catch potential security issues and coding mistakes early in the development cycle.

These appendices provide a quick reference to essential Go commands, common errors, and best practices. By keeping them in mind, you'll be able to maintain cleaner code, quickly diagnose problems, and build more secure and performant Go applications.

www.ingramcontent.com/pod-product-compliance
Lightning Source LLC
LaVergne TN
LVHW051420050326
832903LV00030BC/2924